CW00550981

# Foundry Mill

*My Mother Elsie*

# Betty M. Marson

*BM Marson*

1

Published by Yorkshire Art Circus
All rights reserved. This book or parts thereof cannot be reproduced in any form without permission
Acknowledgements
Thanks to Yorkshire Art Circus Joan Thornton and Steve Truelove
For their help with self-publication.

# Acknowledgements

Robert N. Marson

David Marson and Susan Hawkridge

Dorothy Bowes's extensive Family History spanning five years including night school.

John Gilleghan M.B.E.

Ground work Leeds

Yorkshire Post Leeds

Jeanette Garnett

Leeds Reference Library

Joan Thornton and Steve Truelove from Yorkshire Art Circus

Sadie Healey

The Barwicker

John Smeaton Leeds Reference Library

Barry Crabtree

Christine and Alison Booth

# Contents

.

# Chapter One
# Foundry Mill Farm Seacroft

The Bowes family is shown in standard text and Marson family in italics.

The Family Tree

| | |
|---|---|
| 1680 | Thomas Porter married Elinor Siddle, descendant of Ann Siddle |
| 1714 | Thomas Porter. |
| 1745 | William Porter married Margaret Alderson Father John Alderson. |
| 1765 | Ann Cleminson, William Bowes' Grandmother. |
| 1766 | David Porter married Mary Heslop- Father George, Mother -Mary Shaw. |
| 1785 | Francis George Leathem, Ann Leathem's Father. |
| 1785 | Ann Bowes married George Russell, Catherine Bowes Great Grandfather born 1789 in Castle Bolton. |
| 1785 | John Siddle, Father of Ann Siddle. |
| 1786 | Margaret Porter traced to 1714, Mother of Ann Siddle. |
| 1800 | Mary Lancaster, Mother of Jane Tate. |
| 1805 | Matthew Tate, Father of Jane Tate. |
| 1818 | Thomas Bowes born Downholme, William Bowes Father. |
| 1822 | Ann Siddle [William Bowes Mother] married Thomas Bowes from Elwick 6-1 -1843. |
| 1821 | Francis Leathem Great, great, great Grandfather at Little Ouseburn. |
| 1847 | Ann Leathem born 24 February, married William Bowes in 1868. |
| 1850-1934 | William Bowes born 4th April, Betty's Great-Grandfather at Moorhouse Farm, Farm, Marrick in North Yorkshire. |
| *1867-1960* | *William Henry Marson, born Armley Leeds.* |

| | |
|---|---|
| *1869-1959* | *Lily Sowden, 1881 census shows Father William W Sowden 44yrs, Mother Harriet Sowden 32yrs, Meanwood Leeds, Bob's paternal Grandmother.* |
| *1869-1935* | *Samuel George Naylor 34 Skilbeck Sreet New Wortley (Father James Naylor, a Horse keeper) Bob's maternal Grandpa, his sisters Hannah and Martha, Mother Elizabeth Naylor.* |
| *1873–1961* | *Lucy Maudslay, Father Tom Maudslay, born in Bawtry Yorkshire, Mother Mary Maudslay, born Gawber Yorkshire, brother Harry 13 years, Elizabeth 10 years, Lucy 8 years, Robert 6 years, Emily 3 years, Tom Maudslay Compositor, sister Emily Maudslay brother-in-law Donald Lennox, Bob's maternal Grandmother.* |
| 1874-1926 | Catherine Bowes, born Thorner, Betty's paternal Grandmother Father William Bowes, Mother Ann Leathem. |
| *1880-1962* | *Lucy Naylor (Maudslay) Bob's Grandmother born Armley.* |
| 1891-1956 | Alice Britton, my Mother's sister, Alice was born at The Grange Gambles Thorpe to Alburn and Ada Britton my maternal Grandparents. Shirley and Keith lived in her house in Dewsbury Road after she died. |
| 1894 | Glennis Reuben Roberts my Dad's brother born 15th January at The Gatehouse, Stockfield Lane Scholes. He was in the Grenadier Guards and the Police Force. He married Dolly from Hereford. Sons, John 1921, William and Glen 1927. |
| *1898-1978* | *Rowland Marson born 22 May, died July 1978, Bob's father.* |
| 1901-1965 | Aubrey Henry Robert Bowes, born 29th May, [Betty's Father], at the Toll Bar Whinmoor. |
| 1903-1977 | Dennis Osborn, born Mayfield Farm married Violet, Son Dennis, Daughters Marlene and Sheila. |
| *1906-1987* | *Dorothy Mary (Naylor) Marson, born 17th May, Bob's Mother.* |

| | |
|---|---|
| 1907-1964 | Elsie Britton (Bowes) Born on the seventh March. Betty, Dorothy, Shirley and Tommy's Mother born 60 The Green Seacroft. |
| 1926 | William Osborn, Step-Grandfather to Betty, of Mayfield Farm Seacroft died 9th July, killed by lightning. |
| 1926-1874 | Catherine (Bowes) Osborn died 23rd November, Betty's Grandmother |
| *1932-1996* | *John Marson Bob's brother married Joan Millard son Richard 1964, Heather 1972, a Downs Syndrome. Richard married Tracey Jowett, daughter Lauren 1995 and son Sam 1997.* |
| 1932-1996 | Dorothy Bowes born August 2, Foundry Mill Farm Seacroft. |
| 1934 | Betty Margaret (Bowes) Marson born 18th December. |
| 1939 | Thomas Aubrey Bowes born 5th May, Mount Pleasant Farm. |
| *1936* | *Robert Naylor Marson, born 11 April, married Betty Bowes in 1957, son David 1961, daughter Susan 1963. David married Lynn Butler in 1984, daughters Kirsty 6-3-1986 and Jessica 11-9-1990. Susan married David Hawkridge 1986, son Christopher 13-8-1988, daughter Amanda Claire 18-9-1990.* |
| 1937 | Shirley Anne Bowes, born 6 August, married Keith Booth born 1933, in 1956. Daughters Christine 1961 Alison 1963, son Andrew in 1965. Keith Booth's Father, Fred Booth born 1890 died in 1951, mother Emily Booth 1892 died 1979 lived Allerton Bywater and Swillington. Alison married Michael Rowan in1985, son Matthew 10-8-1989, daughter Louise 26-12-1991. Andrew married Gail in 1991, daughter Nicole 13-4 1992, son Callum.14-6-1995. |
| 1939-1996 | Thomas Aubrey Bowes born 5 May died 25 May. |
| 1944 | William Bowes, Killed in the war.1st Battalion Grenadier Guards died in Calvados France |

This is the story of two farms, Foundry Mill Farm Seacroft and Mount Pleasant Farm, Swillington. The farms dated back to the 1500's. The land for both farms in the 12th Century belonged to the de Laci family. My father's great-grandparents were William Bowes born 1850, from Moorhouse Farm, Marrick in North Yorkshire and Ann Leathem born 1847. They were married at Great Ouseburn in 1868. William Bowes's father and mother were Thomas Bowes born 3-11-1820 and Ann Siddle born 10-6-1822 in Marrick, North Yorkshire, with ancestors who lived at Downholme. They moved to Yorkshire to find work in the 1800's. Times were hard for the Dalesman even though farming was supplemented by some lead mining. Thomas Bowes my great, great grandfather married a farmer's daughter in 1843 Ann Siddle and after his death, his two sons, John and William, eventually moved with their mother, five miles from Barwick to Thorner.

John and William Bowes both married local girls from Bardsey and Shadwell. After a short stay in Roecliffe, William Bowes and his wife Ann (Leathem from Morwick Hall Whinmoor) moved to Whinmoor. William became a platelayer on the railway whilst his wife Ann worked the crossing gates at Scholes (the Railway had been opened in May 1879). The North Eastern Railway opened the branch between Crossgates and Wetherby in 1876, with a station at Scholes, still open in 1910. They lived in the house situated on the footpath to York Road. They were my great grandparents. My grandmother was Catherine, 1874-1926 and her brother was Thomas Bowes with his wife Christina who lived at Pigeoncote Farm at Seacroft. Catherine's sister Jane married Alfred White; their grand daughter married Roy Dixon of Parlington.

My father was born on the 29th May 1901 at the Old Toll Bar Cottage at Scholes and attended Barwick School. In 1901, 191 children were on the roll at Barwick School where the rector was the Reverend Frederick Selincourt Colman from 1899 to 1910, who wrote The History of the Parish of Barwick in Elmet. He started the Parish Magazine and was a great supporter of the Maypole. My father attended the special Whit Mondays when the maypole was raised. The Maypole stands at the centre of the village. It is 90ft tall and one of the tallest in the country. It is taken down every third Easter Monday and carried into the tower field where it is painted and restored. It is painted with red white spiral stripes, blue has been added later. The Maypole was the focal point of Barwick in Elmet. Barwick was mentioned in the Domesday Book as Beruuith meaning a village where barley is grown.

I always remember my father telling us that the teacher had told him that he had common sense and that was as important as being clever. I think he was a very clever man and a good farmer. My father was a handsome popular man with a good personality, but always seemed very strict with us. He lived for a time with Alf White and his Aunt Jinnie who was Catherine's sister; from Barwick and their children son John, (who married Queenie Hemingway, from the family of Heminway butchers, whose twin daughters were Joyce and Barbara.) Ethel (Hemsworth) and her sister Eva (Coates).

My father was the milkman around Foundry Lane and Killingbeck for over thirty years, firstly delivering milk in a pony and trap, ladling the milk out of galvanised gill and pint measuring jugs, into the customers own jug. From Mount Pleasant Farm he bought a van and delivered the milk in glass bottles with cardboard tops.

Catherine, my paternal grandmother, mother of Glennis and Aubrey, my father, married William Osborn in 1904, a widower whose wife had died and he had two daughters, Emily born in 1897 and Elsie born in 1899. William had lived down The Boyle in Barwick. Catherine and William Osborn moved to Mayfield Farm at Seacroft with Glennis, Aubrey and Dennis, born to William and Catherine in 1905.

In 1926 William Osborn was killed by lightning at the open window of Mayfield Farm, watching my father in the field. He was buried in Barwick churchyard where his gravestone shows this fact. For a few months the farm was looked after by Dennis and my father, Glennis was in the Grenadier Guards in London and later joined the Police Force. When Catherine, their mother died shortly after with cancer at 56 years old, Mayfield Farm was given up. Dennis went to live at Whitelaithe Farm, Whinmoor, with his wife Violet and their three children Dennis, Marlene and Sheila. Glennis Bowes lived on Selby Road, Whitkirk, later on Austhorpe Lane. His wife Dolly came from Herefordshire. They had three children John, William, (who was killed in the war), and Glen. The name of William Bowes is on the memorial on the Lytchgate at Whitkirk Church

My mother was born on the 7th march 1907, in a small cottage 60 The Green, Seacroft. It was a very attractive village with a large green where the local cricket matches are played. Her parents were Ada and Alburn Britton from Gamblesforth near Selby. My mother was one of eleven children, two of who died of diphtheria in the epidemic, which struck Seacroft village in May 1928. My maternal grandma Ada was the last grandparent to die when I was about five years old. I missed having grandparents and envied the children at school who could visit them.

My mother married my father in St Mary's Church Seacroft (built in 1845) on April 18th 1931, it was described in the paper as a very pretty wedding. They moved to Foundry Mill Farm. It was situated in a very beautiful rural area with lots of wild flowers in the summer around the Foundry Millponds. There were country footpaths over the fields to Seacroft to see her family, and to Roundhay Park. A bridlepath led to Crossgates from Foundry Lane.

Foundry Mill and Seacroft Iron Works were on Foundry Lane Seacroft, with the Foundry Mills being on the site of the old manorial mills. The Foundry used the Low moor beds of ironstone and coal. The Foundry and corn mills were supplied with water, via a conduit from Wykebeck. The beck and site of the Foundry were west of the current buildings of Seacroft Grange Primary School, which was opened in 1974. The first water wheel was designed by John Smeaton (1724-1792) a famous engineer from Whikirk and educated at Leeds Grammar School. His most famous project was the third Eddystone Lighthouse. His overshot wheel at the Foundry was 30ft in diameter by 4ft-6ins wide, mounted on a massive oak axle. Cast-iron fittings enabled sixteen radiating wooden spokes to support the iron rim. It was used at the time the Foundry was being developed. It drove the coke furnace and an engine that would pump water from the millponds in dry weather.

In June 1792, a Leeds newspaper had a notice for the sale of 'the iron foundry at Seacroft with the engine, waterwheel,

*Ada Britton*
*Maternal Grandma*

*Alburn Britton*
*Paternal Grandpa*

warehouses, shops, two house, six cottages and thirteen acres of land, so it was quite a large concern. The millstones turned by the Smeaton mill wheel produced coarse brown flour. There was a large pond about a hundred yards east of the mill but this was drained later. A map of 1894 marks the 'Millponds' as a reminder, and there are records going back to 1577.

Darcy Bruce Wilson M.A., 1851-1936 the last of the Wilson family to run the Manor of Seacroft, he lived at Seacroft Hall, demolished in 1954. He delighted to show visitors around Foundry Mill and its unusual wheel. When Darcy Wilson died in 1936 the Seacroft estate was sold to Leeds Corporation who served notice in June 1934 to Seacroft Hall, seven farms, cottages, Seacroft Lodge and other lands, that had to be demolished, in order to build the largest council estate in Europe, 7,000 houses built by 1947, by 1965, 40,000 council houses had been built.

When the Foundry mill was demolished in 1937-8 the Smeaton wheel was taken for storage into a council site and after attempts to preserve it, the wheel was broken up, perhaps some parts were taken to the Park Row museum although these were lost in the bombing in March 1941.On the north side of Foundry Lane where Seacroft Grange School is now, once stood a row of picturesque houses, called the Whitehouses that were a delight in the daffodil season. Seacroft Hall stood in Foundry Lane, near the mill, was demolished and the area used to build a Grammar School in 1953, and changed to a Comprehensive School Parklands High, which our daughter Susan attended in 1966-1969.

Foundry Mill Farm Seacroft Leeds was where in the early thirties my sisters Dorothy, an engaging ginger haired little daughter, a very bright child was born 1932, and my sister Shirley who was a merry brown haired little girl, my father always called her "Sha' were born in 1937. And I, Betty

Margaret Bowes was born in 1934. I was born with a veil over my head called a caul, which was much desired by sailors, because it meant that they would not drown. I do not know whether the midwife sold mine or not. My brother Thomas was born in 1939 at Mount Pleasant Farm. My earliest memory of Foundry Mill is of some boys throwing sticks for the conkers, near the mill, and me pinching the small pile of shiny conkers and running as fast as I could home. I also recall my sister Dorothy having earache in a bed with brass bed knobs and I suppose my mother put warm olive oil in her ear to stop the pain.

My mother was Elsie, a lovely small quiet, plump, smiling person, loved by everyone. I have never met another person I have admired more, she was everything a mother should be and we were so lucky she was always there for us, with a huge welcoming smile. My friend Margaret, after reading this story said 'your mother was the best, she was so warm and friendly, and to outsiders a real mum'. I can't remember her hugging us but we felt her love care and concern for all our lives, wrapping around us like a warm blanket. My mother attended the school at Seacroft on the Green. We have a beautifully illustrated book from Sunday school with her name inside. After she left school she went to work for the Sandy Family who lived at Halton, to look after their children. I met one of the children from the Sandy family and she had fond memories of my mother reading stories to her. Every August in the early twenties, the Sandy family took a cottage at Flamborough on the East Coast for the month of August. They were very happy times for my mother, she often spoke of the lovely summers she had there. My parents lived at Foundry Mill Farm for seven years. In 1934 they were given notice to quit by the Leeds City Council. It must have upset my mother to leave such a pretty place and all her friends.

# Chapter Two
# Mount Pleasant Farm

My father Aubrey Bowes of Foundry Mill Farm, Seacroft agreed on the 1st January 1938 to take over the tenancy of Mount Pleasant Farm. He paid Mr. Dawson of Towton, £140 rent per annum for the land, house and buildings. I never met Mr. Dawson, but he had the shooting rights and appeared at the end of the drive with his friends in autumn, to shoot the many pheasants, rabbits and hares on the land.

In 1939 we left Foundry Mill Farm and we moved into the very pretty Mount Pleasant Farm, which had been part of Swillington House estate. The farm was situated halfway between Garforth Bridge and Swillington on Wakefield Road. The history of the land around the farm has always interested me. Opposite the farm gate was Mount Pleasant Pit opened in 1893, the square tower of the winding lift stood proudly as a landmark. It is now a picnic area. At either side of the large iron entrance gates were two stags on pillars brought from Swillington House when it was demolished in 1952 due to coal-mining subsidence. It's ironic that the mining that helped to create the wealth led to the subsidence and eventual demolition of Swillington House. However the stables at Swillington House still exist and have been converted into a home. When Bower's the mining firm, started mining there was a gentlemen's agreement not to mine under the church but that did not extend to Swillington House.

It was Sir Charles William Lowther, 4th Baronet (1880-1949) who sold Swillington House, Great and Little Preston Halls and surrounding property and collieries in 1920, after three hundred years of Lowther ownership, mostly to the

Bowers family. Coal has been mined in Swillington since the 17th century and families from the Durham and South Wales collieries moved in to mine the coal. New houses were built along Wakefield Road and Astley Lane for the families and the population of Swillington doubled from 866 to 1,732 in 1891. Primrose Hill Colliery, which connected to Mount Pleasant pit, opened in 1893 closed in 1970. The Mount Pleasant site is now a picnic area.

Farming has always been an important industry in Swillington and until mining developed there was only a church, village school, almshouses and scattered farmhouses and cottages. In 1791 a pottery was situated on the west bank of the river Aire near Swillington House. It produced cream coloured earthenware and 'stone- china'. Sir John Lowther bought it out because he objected to the smoke from the kilns blowing across his property. Current industry in the lands close to Mount Pleasant farm includes Marshall brick making and the production of specialist oils and paints from Rocol. Mount Pleasant Farm is still a working farm owned by the Chapmans family from Austhorpe Hall.

When Mr. Bowers offered the estate for auction in 1935; there were altogether twelve farms, many smallholdings and over 100 cottages as well as Little Preston Hall. Mr Dawson from Towton Hall bought Mount Pleasant Farm. An advertisement for the sale of the land that appeared in papers all over England, showed Lot 35:

'A useful Dairy and Mixed Farm known as Mount Pleasant Farm situated on the Wakefield and York Road and six miles from Leeds. The Farmhouse is brick built and contains a Dining room, Sitting Room, Kitchen, Store Room, and square pantry with a north facing window, four Bedrooms, and Wash House. The brick built farm buildings include Mistals for 29 cows, Dairy, Meal House, six stall Stable, Granary, Barn, Loose Box,

Cartsheds, and Implement shed. Adjoining the Farmhouse is a Sterilising House in which is a Plant, which has been installed by the tenant. The total area of the holding is 135acres - Letting price 136 pounds 6 shillings. Water is laid on. Two cottages at Blackwells are sold with this farm a total of 135 acres.'

Mr Bowers also sold Well Green Farm, the land adjoining Mount Pleasant, to Mr. Dawson of Towton Hall Tadcaster. The previous farmer was Alfred Elam and my father took the tenancy over in March 1941. Well Green Farm had 206 acres and the rent was £203 per annum. The farmhouse was stone built and Mr. Linley moved in to manage the farm along with Foster Darley who later moved to Brecks Lane Farm. Dick Linley had worked at Carters farm at Whinmoor before he came to Garforth Bridge. Well Green Farm, was set in beautiful countryside and there was a pathway to Brecks Farm, that led through Brecks Wood and it was filled with bluebells in spring. Down Cramby Hill, the local name for the section of Wakefield Road that goes from Mount Pleasant Farm to Well Green Farm, had hedgerows sheltering peeping violets, which we looked for every spring.

On the agreement that my father signed to take over Mount Pleasant Farm on the 1st January 1938 the following list was agreed from the outgoing tenant Norman Armitage. 'An away going crop of corn off one fourth part of the arable land such crop to be sown on land which shall have been summer fallow, turnips, mangolds, potatoes in the preceding summer, provided that the land sown after potatoes shall not exceed more than one third of the total away going crop. The crop, grain only, to be valued immediately prior to harvest, subject to one years rent and taxes. The cost of the clover seeds sown in the spring of the previous year provided the seed was of good quality and sown in the first corn crop after fallow. The fair value of the hay and straw, the produce of the holding in the preceding summer, which shall have been left, unconsumed. It had 75 acres of Arable land and 49 acres of grass with 39acres of plain lands to homestead. The rent was 140 pounds, 125acres.'

The brick farmhouse was built in two parts, the oldest with low ceilings and small windows dating back to before the 1800's. A new part built onto the old farm buildings, overlooked the orchard and Swillington, and had three airy bedrooms with large sash windows. A bathroom had been installed in a bedroom in the old part and a wide staircase added. It had a shiny, smooth wooden banister we could slide down. There were beautiful views from all the windows. The farm was so high and my favourite view was from the top bedroom window. I could see Holme Moss on a clear day and the spire of St Mary's Church Swillington peeping over the trees of the Rectory, with green fields full of cows grazing in the fields towards Nicholls Farm on Swillington Lane. My mother's room was a large sunny bedroom. It had a little closet in the corner where my mother kept her dainty high-heeled shoes she had got married in and a concertina we loved to try and play.

There was a long drive from the farm to Wakefield Road, quite visible from the kitchen window. It was bordered each side with hedgerows laden in summer with sweet smelling pink and white wild roses and the chattering of the sparrows. On the left hand side was the pond where in spring we searched for the small black-wriggling tadpoles, lots of frogspawn and the many little fish darting about. The drive looks quite different now as tall trees border the drive. We had another pond in the fields nearer to Swillington, close to Bear Park Cottages, where we looked for the bright yellow water blobs in the summer. Bear Park Cottages, where my friend Derreen Linley lived after they left Well Green Farm, had a fresh water spring. Along the hedgerows in the fields, the brightly coloured pheasants raised their young and went scattering away when we ran past. We looked for the pale mauve milkmaids and cowslips and picked mushrooms in the fields below the farm. There was a footpath over the stile at the gate past the pond, over to Swillington Lane across the gardens of Mr Smith the coalman to Templenewsam. There were many people crossing the fields on a summer Sunday.

Past the pond and a slight incline up was the mistal where my father had thirty-three cows to be milked twice a day. It was a large long building, cosy and warm in winter. What a sight it was in spring, after weeks inside the cows were let out into the fields and ran kicking their heels. Everyone came out to watch them; they did make my father laugh. In summer I used to bring them up from the second field below the farm, with the two dogs Lassie and Floss. I used to shout 'coos, coos' and the cows used to look up and follow the dogs that rounded them up in convoy into the cowshed.

The cows were all tethered down the right hand side of the mistal with feeding troughs and a cut out in the floor for the waste matter to run out into the field. I fell into this dirty stream when I was about eight and was scolded, put straight into the bath, scrubbed clean and told how dangerous it was to fall into it. Adjoining the mistal was the diary where the milk was bottled. It was a cold job in winter. A stone floor in that building that could be swilled with hot water. The milk went down the cooler before being poured into bottles and cardboard tops pressed on. In the corner was a huge galvanised bath where the bottles were washed before putting back into the crates waiting to be filled.

In the red-bricked farmhouse, the kitchen and the first room looked down the drive bordered by a rectangular yard. Laddie, a sheepdog was fastened up all day outside the kitchen door, in a kennel with just enough lead to let people into the house. He guarded the front of the house and barked with furious intent at the many cats that tried to get into the house and washhouse. The cats never came into the house because the house dogs ginger haired Floss and wirehaired Lassie chased them out. There was a huge commotion if a tiny field mouse showed its face. Lassie, who followed me everywhere, and Floss sat under the kitchen table, we were not supposed to feed them but we managed to feed them our crusts. My Father bought Lassie when we were quite small and when she was able to have puppies we used to keep her in, but she always managed to get out to Laddie who was fastened up outside the kitchen door and the resultant pups which arrived, made beautiful sheepdog pups much to our delight. They were born and kept in the barn. When my mam and dad went out we brought them into the kitchen where they wet all over the clipped rugs.

The huge ancient barn was where the owls lived, and sat in the moonlight on a ledge high up on the side of the barn, hooting away. The corn was stored on the upper level of the barn at the bottom of the yard, up the steps to see the huge mound of golden sweet smelling corn. There was a place in the yard to keep a pig, which my father killed at Christmas and divided out amongst the relatives and friends, after the pig had been killed in the washhouse, the pig salted and kept in the cellar, Mam baked stand pies made with hot water pastry, the brawn mixed in the huge yellow mixing bowl. It always seemed to be fall on the night for Handel's Messiah and we joined in the chorus's with gusto with the special favourites "I know that my Redeemer liveth and the 'Alleluia' chorus. Dorothy usually came home from the hospital where she was training to be with us on that night, often she had to work all over Christmas.

# Chapter Three
# The Farmhouse Kitchen

The kitchen door led into a very sunny room, one window looking down the yard to the main road and the back window, looked north on to a hill with a hedgerow filled with bluebells in spring and blackberries in autumn. My father watched through the back window of the kitchen for game and if he saw the pheasants, rabbits or hares, he would fetch his gun. After it had been killed the game would hang in the back place for a few days. The back place was a small room off the kitchen, which had an unused staircase that led up to mine, and Shirley's bedroom. We had game for dinner every week. We loved the rich gravy from the rabbits, the meat so rich, but most of all, our favourite was the stuffing made from homemade bread, onions, mixed herbs, suet and eggs. Bacon and ham joints were also hung in the back place. When bluebottles got to these joints and laid their eggs my mother cut away that part, peppered the joints and hung them back up.

The bright sunny kitchen was a square large room, a huge glowing coal fire in the black-leaded Yorkist range, with a good oven, the temperature controlled by how much heat from the fire. A raised grate near the fire, the pans and kettle placed on it and the steamer, which cooked the potatoes and vegetables at the same time. The fire was used to heat the water in the large cylinder in the bathroom upstairs and a brass topped fireguard in front to keep us safe, and a large mantle shelf above it where spiders dropped into your hair as we were cooking. Our breakfast consisted of bread fried with dripping from the meat, baked beans and fried eggs. The kitchen was where we lived most of the time being the warmest place. Five large clipped rugs on the stone kitchen floor. My mother made the clipped rugs on a large Hessian covered frame from strips of old wool coats pushed through the material with a wooden pointed piece of wood and then pulled back through another hole pulled together until they were level and the back neat, and the front worked to a pattern They were very warm to stand on but they were very heavy to lift and to shake the dust from them.

A large square scrubbed topped table in the centre, a place for homework, it was covered with a red velvet cloth when the white tablecloth used for meals, was removed. There were two sideboards in the kitchen and a small grandfather clock ticking away on the wall. The sweet aroma of homemade bread and baking, filling the kitchen with the smell of home.

My mother filled the paraffin lamp each morning from the paraffin kept in the washhouse, carrying it very carefully not to break the fragile mantle. It gave a lovely glow set on the red tablecloth on the kitchen table; the farmhouse in winter was very dark. When we went to bed we had to use candles. There

*Aubrey and Elsie Bowes .*
*My Mother and Father*

21

were other paraffin lamps in the first room and the far room. We had the blue Willow pattern design tea-set kept on the left of the fireplace and the silverfish darted away when the cupboard was opened and if we broke a cup it was replaced from Pease's shop at Garforth.

My father sat in the large chair at the left hand side of fireplace. His meals had to be ready on the dot of twelve and five o'clock with drinks of tea at ten and three o'clock. My mother always sat at the right hand side of the fireplace with a footstool to rest her legs on. My mother suffered with arthritis and varicose veins. We had cushions on the wooden chairs but they were not very comfortable. My mother did not have an easy life, with the house full of people to feed, four children, and Land Girls extra. My mother enjoyed making a fuss of everyone but she had no favourites amongst the four children. My mother was always keeping the peace between my father and us, as we were a lively mischievous lot, always giggling and joking, chasing each other round the table. I never heard her grumble, always pleasant and smiling. She loved company and the minute people came down the drive to the farm, the shout went up 'put the kettle on' as everyone stayed for a while. My mother bought many of her clothes at Walkers in Leeds where the money was taken in a brass pipe for the change and sent back down much to our amazement. Mam liked to dress smartly and when money was available, she went into Leeds to buy a new coat and hat. She was never more fashionable than at Shirley and Keith's wedding in a very smart, navy suit. My mother was always spotlessly clean and always changed at teatime, with a bright clean apron. My mother had chickens at the top of the garden, the sale from the eggs being her pin money. Funnily enough I cannot remember any foxes getting them. I'm afraid I did not like collecting the eggs because I always came back with a flea; they never seemed to bother my mother.

On a Sunday, my mother and father's friends, Myers's and Garsides's came. The red velvet tablecloth came out, the pennies and the cards, and amidst lots of laughter we played card games. Great hilarity, when we were playing Newmarket if when all the cards were turned over and all the pennies on the last card, you could lose two shillings if you were unlucky, but money for pictures if you won. We put the 'snow' sixpences underneath the tablecloth. We had Tizer to drink and Quality Street sweets passed around. These special friends supported my parents when Thomas had the accidents and had to be in hospital for so long. My mother loved to go to Swillington church to the beautiful evening service with familiar old hymns played by Tom Noble on the organ, and would hurry Sunday tea, to walk the long road to church with my aunts and cousins, Audrey, Irene and Dorothy. Sometimes in summer the church doors were left open letting in the sunshine and warmth.

In the large bathroom, above the kitchen, were two sideboards as well as the bath, sink and a huge cylinder for hot water heated by the coalfire. It kept the bathroom and our little bedroom over the kitchen warm. My mother and father's bedroom had a fireplace in it too. The front room of the house was a very large and sunny room, facing the yard and drive with huge sash windows, one looking onto the garden and another looking over the orchard which was filled with apple and pear trees. There used to be a huge pear tree that was struck by lightning, but still produced loads of pears, despite the stricken branch fallen to the ground. The garden was my father's pride and joy, with rows of beautiful home-grown vegetables including sweet tasting potatoes, green beans, cabbages, broad beans, rhubarb onions and beetroot sowed in neat rows in the garden with plenty of manure. They never seem to taste as sweet and tender today as they did then. Flowers grew under the window and we had a lovely plum tree set in the middle of the garden. On the outside of the front room window pane Derreen and I saw the largest spider we have ever seen and when we poked it the spider sent a stream of water out. It is still a talking point to this day.

The large rolled topped pine desk stood in the corner of the front room, where my father kept the farm's accounts. A huge oak sideboard stood at the opposite side of the room, very ornate piece of furniture, with three large mirrors and carvings over the top, I would have loved to take it when Bob and I got married but our house was too small.

A shiny polished oak table stood in the middle of that room, it had a special handle to make a space for extra leaves, to

*Bob and Betty's Wedding with Aubrey and Elsie Bowes Lucy Naylor Thomas, John Marson Right hand side of the bride.*
*William and Lily Marson. Rowland and Dorothy Marson Left hand side*

extend the table for parties, and large enough to have a game of table tennis. How we loved that table, it was used to play houses under it, play post offices with miniature letters and stamps, but most of all we put a cushion and slid all over it. The table was the centre for the many parties, especially at Christmas when I had a birthday party with all my friends. The last party before the farm was given up was our David's christening in 1963.

We had an oak wind up gramophone, which we played for hours and danced to the music. I can remember 'Rose's From the South' and 'Dancing Cheek to Cheek'. Later I had the records from the musical South Pacific. We played with miniature cardboard shops with small glass jars of sweets of dolly mixtures and cashews. The hall was where the telephone was situated and we could ring our friends for as long as we liked for 4d. A red carpet ran the length of the hall down to the huge heavy front door, seldom opened to the garden.

To the right of this door was the far room, holding the piano. It had a coalfire, but not lit every day, so it was often too cold to practice the piano in before electricity was put in the farm, the year before Shirley got married. My father promised us a ten-shilling note each when we could play Home Sweet Home. Needless to say we practised until we could play it and to this day I can still play the opening bars. Dorothy was the most proficient and played Tchaichovsky 's 'Piano Concerto Number One'. Shirley loved to play 'Bells Across the Meadow', and I could play Chopin's 'Nocturne in E major'. The piano filled the house with music and echoed down the hall. We attended classes with Mrs Winters who lived at opposite the church at Swillington. My father liked it best when my aunts and uncles came and we sang all the old tunes. His favourites were 'Down at the Old Bull and Bush' and Harry Lauder's songs.

Along the front of the house that faced down towards Swillington was the garden path running towards the toilet and henhouses, a long dark walk in winter. In the house there was the daily ritual of emptying the potties into a bucket and taking down the garden to empty it in the earth toilet and the potties washed. An earth toilet with two holes side by side, scrubbed clean, the toilet paper cut in squares of newspaper from the Yorkshire Post hung behind the door. What a very beautiful view down the fields to Swillington, from out of that door with no one to see you, but if you could hear the rattle of the back outside door, we made a very quick exit, as it meant the council men had come to empty it.

All day the kitchen wireless was tuned into the lovely music of the Light programme. There was Geraldo's orchestra complete with singers on a Friday afternoon. Favourite songs were Jo Stafford's lovely song 'The Shrimp Boats are a Coming,' Guy Mitchell's 'Singing The Blues,' Frankie Laine's 'Jezebel,' 'Oh Mine Papa' and 'Answer Me.' Family Favourites started the day, followed at lunchtime with Workers' Playtime, with many of the comedians alive today including Greengrass from Heartbeat, a popular programme set in Goathland on the television today. At two o'clock we listened to Woman's Hour with talks and discussions on everyday situations. A serial was read at the end, my favourite a Naomi Jacob book. There was Force's Favourite on a Sunday with Jean and Cliff Michelmore, Grand Hotel with orchestral music on at eight o'clock on a Sunday night when we came home from church. Housewives Choice was a lovely programme that ran from 1946-1967. In the morning, Mrs Dale's Diary from 1948 to 1969 broadcast every day at four fifteen. I still listened to it after we were married.

Music While You Work, every show came from a different factory canteen 'Some where in England' at lunchtimes we listened to when my father came in for dinner that we had at mid day, with the theme tunes Calling All Workers by Eric Coates. The compere was Bill Gates while Jack Clarke and George Middleton played the piano. Regular favourites were Elsie and Doris Waters. The last show was on the 6th October 1964. It starred Anne Shelton, Cyril Fletcher, and Val Doonican a singer we admired. This wonderful wartime started as a Saturday show on May 24th, 1941 and soon moved up to lunchtimes three times a week. The wireless ran on accumulators, which, when they ran down, there was much despair when the sound started to disappear and we had to get new ones from Garforth. We listened to Radio Luxemburg much to my father's disgust, modern music a bit of a crackly reception too. There were lots of flies in summer my mother would use 'Flit' and sweep them up afterwards. We had sticky trips hanging down too, to catch the flies.

The farmhouse and farmyard was always busy with the Land girls and people calling to buy potatoes, corn and farm matters. I was told that my father was an excellent farmer and with Dick Linley as the manager who was one of the best ploughmen around, they farmed the land well. My father looked with envy at the farmland of the Wolds, he thought it was such rich farmland it would have been more productive to farm.

My father had been seriously ill with Pneumonia when we were children, he had Nurse Commander from Swillington, who scared us as children, but became a good friend to me, when I was at the dressmaking class at Swillington School, when I was eighteen years old. My father had a fire lit in the bedroom and was very weak after the illness; we could hear his breathing downstairs. It was said that he only had one lung working.

When we were poorly we had a spoonful of Fennings Fever cure, it had a bitter taste. At school some children had to line up for cod liver oil and malt but I hated the taste. Our favourite food, when we were poorly, was Robinson's Groats mixed with milk, treacle and cream added, similar to porage, it was kept as a treat, and sure to make us feel better. We never had it any other time.

Christmas was always a busy time for my mother. My father's cousins Ethel and Eva would buy us colouring books and pencils as they worked at Arnolds in Leeds. My mother baked Christmas cakes, mince pies with lots of lovely smells. I remember the postman coming on Christmas morning, chasing the Land Girls around the table for a kiss. Our relatives and friends coming to tea, and we attended the Christmas services at St Mary's Swillington. It was a lovely homely warm happy time.

# Chapter Four
# Childhood

Shirley Tommy and I played hide and seek around the farm buildings, but not in the stackyard because my father said it was dangerous, he considered horses were very dangerous near children too. The large enclosed well-drained yard made a great place for tennis, Shirley and I played together, just knocking the tennis ball backwards and forwards to each other. We played hopscotch on the stone flagged path outside the kitchen door and games with two small tennis balls throwing them onto a wall and catching them. Tommy played with marbles and conkers. We skipped with a huge rope reciting rhymes, Silk, Satin, Muslin and Lace over and over until the skipping rope caught you. Shirley and I loved to see how long we could stand on our hands with our feet against the wall. I remember getting up very early one morning taking a blanket and both of us trying to see who could stay up on our hands the longest. We had a small rooftop near the front room window, we dressed up in old net curtains and sang and danced. Also games of whip and top, where you painted a pattern on the top hit it with a whip and watched it go the round.

Thomas was always breaking windows and kept Mr. Getting, joiner and undertaker who lived down Swillington Lane busy mending them. An old bill from him was £3 19s for repairs to floors and a cart. Thomas' favourite game was cricket. We played cricket for hours, good practice for Shirley and I when we were in the Ladies cricket team in Swillington and played the Ladies team from Allerton Bywater. The wireless in summer was tuned to the cricket and those famous commentators John Arlot and Brian Johnston remind me of those days.

We were so far away from Swillington we did not have friends to play with, and in the main got on very well, and we remained very good friends all our lives, and even when we were married we saw each other every week. We had a magical childhood, we all had bicycles to ride up and down the drive and rode everywhere on them, as we were nearly a mile from Swillington and Garforth Bridge. We were able to leave the bicycles behind the café at Garforth Bridge and in Mr. Templeman's house at Swillington. Margaret Templeman was Shirley's friend who was in the same class at Rothwell Grammar School. We had always to wash the pots and then we could go out to play. The old coal place near the kitchen door later made into the flush toilet was our playroom when we were little; we made pretend meals from Colact a kind of drink and rhubarb raw from the garden

When Thomas was little, he had been playing with the handle of the tennis racket in the front room fire, and dropped it on the settee, where it smouldered, we were sleeping in the bedroom up above, it was very frightening as smoke was pouring from the front room, but my dad opened the windows and told us everything was alright.

When Tommy was a baby we all had measles, I was the first to catch it, I was reading by the firelight and my mother saw the rash. It was always said the measles caused the damage to my eyes that I have always worn glasses, from thirteen years of age. Doctor Smith told my mother to put the beds in the far room because we should all catch it. The curtains were drawn for days, and it was quite a serious illness in those days. We also had Chicken Pox.

Shirley badly scalded her foot, it came up in a large blister, after she jumped down into a hot water filled bucket, which the Land Girls had filled to wash the milk bottles in the dairy. Tommy had a bad scald on his arm when the pan slipped on the fire. They both had dressings of paraffin gauze that healed the scalds. Dorothy had Scarlet Fever and went to Garforth Cliff Isolation Hospital, I had Yellow Jaundice and Scarlet Fever, and Tommy had nasty weeping knees from falling off his bike. Doctor Smith from Crossgates was so good to us. I

*Swillington Primary School*

*Swillington Sportsday*

cannot remember anyone having an upset stomach, quite the reverse. There was the weekly spoonful of Syrup of Figs. My mother had a little red book for all the ailments we had as children. The little red book came out and to our great amusement the book said, after giving advice, you had to keep your bowels open with the medicine they were selling.

My dad kept the marshmallow ointment for the cattle and dogs, not us though, according to my dad it was the cure for everything. My dad was very caring and spoilt us when we were poorly. We used to catch the Wakefield to Garforth bus that ran every two hours, and stayed in Garforth twenty minutes to do our shopping, it was risk that if we missed the bus, we had to walk home from Garforth Bridge up Cramby hill with the heavy shopping. We bought lovely Sally Lunns and Vanilla slices from Freeman's shop. Mrs. Freeman also catered for Shirley and Keith in 1956 and Bob and I in 1957 when were married. The cost was ten shillings and sixpence a head, and the wedding receptions were both held in the Welfare Hall Swillington, after the service at Saint Mary's Church Swillington.

# Chapter Five
# Schooldays

I started Swillington School on my fifth birthday, 18th December1939 and it was Christmas time, and I was thrilled to bits with it all and was given a soft blue doll that I treasured. The primary teacher was Miss Fozzard, who lived in a lovely cottage on Rattan Row Swillington Lane. Miss Fozzard had been given an award for teaching 22 years in 1922, so by the time we went she had been teaching nearly forty years. She was so popular and we loved her. We were given a slate and chalk and we had to write, 'the cat sat on the mat '. My father had taught us to write our own names before we went to school and I remember helping the other children. We had a soft boat swing to play on that was kept on a shelf.

There were three classes at the little school and the next teacher was Miss Stead, we bought magic painting books (we were amazed at the colours appearing when we tried them in

*Rothwell Grammar School Class with Dorothy and Betty*

33

the small sinks in the small cloakroom near the classroom) from Mrs. Hartwells, who had the shop at the top of Church Lane; a farthings worth of sweets and Lucky Bags with sherbet and Liquorice sticks. There were four farthings in a penny; we had a penny to spend three times a week.

In 1941 when children were seven they moved to Miss Bellwood's class, a small plump lady from Castleford, there was a large stove in this class room and on cold mornings we put our coats on the pipes and did exercises to keep warm. The ice on the milk was melted on the pipes but spoilt the milk. The older children were milk monitors, the ink monitors filled the inkwells. A new pen nib was issued for exams. There was a large stove in this classroom. There were three pictures on the wall, one of a boy blowing bubbles painted by Millais the famous Pears soap advertisement, at the moment in Leeds Art Gallery, part of the Unilever Group collection, and the other [Gainsborough Print] of a man pointing out to sea, with two small boys, and a picture of The Owl and the Pussycat going to sea. I got the cane in that class; you had to hold your hand straight out, afterwards the cane left a weal on your palm. It really hurt and brought tears to your eyes.

We had to write compositions and do arithmetic, we had some instruments to play and I especially liked the cymbal. We could write in an exercise book our own stories. At playtime we played games, a favourite was "Poor Mary Lies a Weeping" and the game of Rounders was enjoyed. I remember a family having T.B. and it was a very serious illness. The toilets were in the schoolyard, very cold open topped places. The boys' toilet had no doors either

We had a long walk to school every morning, there was a bus every two hours from Garforth to Wakefield, so we caught it at twelve o clock, had our dinner and walked back nearly a mile to school. When we were at the little school we were encouraged to save Bank money which the teacher took in small amounts on a Monday and when we had saved a pound it went into The Penny Bank at the Post Office owned by Mr. Street, situated down Astley Lane. The interest on the Yorkshire Penny Bank was two shillings on five pounds.

If there was an air raid, we had to go to Mr. Street's shop as we lived too far away from home. Thankfully we never had to. Gas masks were called Razzas for children because of the noise of the breathing. There were special ones for babies. I remember the convoys of soldiers travelling down Wakefield road.

The children moved up to the big school nicknamed 'The Tin Shed' when they were eight years old, to Miss Longbottoms class a much stricter class, she had a board with the Times Table written on it and had the class reciting the tables parrot fashion, often when someone had been naughty, we missed the playtime and the penalty was the times table. Needless to say most of her pupils could recite them now, without having to think about it. It paid off because we had a great proportion of children that went to Grammar Schools from Swillington.

The school needed another classroom, so we were in the Welfare Hall, called The Institute at Swillington, it was next to the Recreation Ground, there was a roundabout, a teapot lid and a slide, we could use at playtimes. There were two classes in the big hall. We played tennis and cricket in the Welfare playing fields all our teenage years. Swillington had Sports days with a Queen, chosen during a special social at the Welfare Hall, with races and competitions for each age group every summer. There was a stage in the Welfare Hall and the song, Greensleeves always reminds me of that time that the children put on a show in 1943. Mrs. Howarth, the teacher a favourite with all the pupils, taught us poems, Wordsworth's 'The Daffodils', and 'The Highwayman' that poem, always made us think of the rhododendron walk from Bullerthorpe Lane to

Templenewsam. The story of 'The Children of the New Forest' was read to us, a book I can remember, visiting The New Forest reminded me of those lessons.

There were two classes in the hall. I remember getting the cane again for talking in class in an exam, because we were going to the baths after school, for the first time to Castleford and I was so excited. We went to sit the eleven plus exam, at the Garforth Barley Hill School and I was so nervous. I

remember writing about the story of a penny, and where it had spent its life. I found the maths problems, ('if John ran so fast in this

*Swillington Church*

*Swillington Rectory*

*Betty, Derreen and Dad*

time, and Robert ran this distance') so hard. In 1944 Eleven plus Exam Children who did not pass to go to the Grammar School, had another chance to go to Castleford Grammar School, or at thirteen to go to the Technical College at Whitwood.

I was a borderline case and had to wait for a place, until the October holidays. I stayed at Swillington School in Miss Gallimore's class from August to October before they found me a place at Normanton High School. Miss Gallimore was very kind to my friend Dorothy from Home Farm enabling her to pass the eleven plus exam, to Normanton High School. The school nicknamed the Tin Hut because the roof was made of corrugated iron, the rain made such a din on the roof. The Head teacher Mr. Silverwood stood up in Assembly one morning and told us not to be frightened of coming to school. The lessons consisted of gardening for the boys on a special allotment where the Cloisters, and Harold Swift's shop is now, and sewing for the girls. There was a drawer full of books that I read at every opportunity. Books were like gold then, the books were about Ancient Britain and the Invasion from the Danes.

My father had a friend called Mr Boddy, whose daughter attended a private school. He brought us a large box of her books when he immigrated to Africa and the books were a mixture of encyclopaedias and children's books, we could not have been given anything better. The old encyclopaedia contained all the knowledge we needed for school. I still remember the information in that book for the quiz programmes, and now battered and torn it helps my grandchildren with their homework. An interesting fact in the book is an article of how brilliant and safe asbestos was, but how dangerous it has now been found to be.

I still enjoy reading and read many books in my teens, but

I am still no good at arithmetic. Children had to leave school at 14yrs, but the law was changed later to 15yrs.

I was so glad that a place was found for me at Normanton High School. In the autumn of 1945, the next school term started on January 10th to April 4th and spring term started April 30th and ended August 1st. We had a very nice school uniform. It was a very old school with lots of oak panelling. The lessons were so interesting and stimulating I was taught about Mesopotamia in the History lessons, and the fact that they put the male babies on the roof, all through the cold night, to ensure that they only had the healthy males left me horrified. We played netball. My form teacher was D. Sever and the headmistress was K.Reeve. The journey to school entailed a bicycle ride, a bus to Castleford and a change to the bus to Normanton. It was very tiring and meant that I had to set off very early in the morning, just after seven. My father worried about the dark mornings and long days, because of this, my father obtained me a place at Rothwell Grammar School.

I stayed at Rothwell Grammar School from Easter 1946-1949. It was founded in 1933 and served the areas of Swillington Rothwell, Lofthouse and surrounding villages. The school was a red-bricked building set in large grounds with rugby pitches and tennis courts. We had a long lunch hour and it was a treat to sit out or play tennis on those beautiful lawns. There was also a wood that we could walk round at playtime. The classrooms were set round a rectangle with a large hall that took all the pupils for Assembly first thing. I enjoyed the hymns and prayers. The pupils were very quiet and attentive and very rarely naughty and if they were, had to see the Head teacher Mr. Manley. I cannot remember anyone having the cane in class. The motto on our blazers was 'Nec Sperno, Nec Timeo', translated to 'I despise nothing, I fear nothing'. We all had to wear cream panama hats and green ties. On the first day I promptly followed my sister Dorothy into her class where she had started in 1945-1949, where the average age was three year older. I stayed in that class and coped with the lessons, I expect with much help from Dorothy.

The snow of 1947 meant we missed many days of school, the farm was snowed in, and the roads were impassable. We caught the Wakefield bus at eight o clock every school morning, outside the farm gate on Wakefield Road near the pit gates and it took an hour to travel through Woodlesford and Rothwell and Outwood to the school at East Ardsley, and if that bus did not run we had, a mile walk to the village, to catch the Castleford bus from there, through the pretty village of Woodlesford.

I was the youngest girl in my year, and I had to present the Lady Mayoress of Wakefield with a bouquet of flowers. I enjoyed the lessons in architecture, which were included in the art lessons on a Friday and looked at churches and buildings in a new light. We had outdoor art lessons in the wood, drawing the vegetation. On the last day of term the History teacher made us sit on chairs around the room and if you answered a question correctly, you went to the top of the class. It was questions like who invented the Steam engine (-James Watt), or who created the road network-(Thomas Telford 1757-1834 and John Mc Adam in 1700's.) We certainly remembered the answers, years later. A bit like the Fifteen to One quiz programme on T.V. at the moment. In Geography as well as learning about England, we went into detail about South America and Australia. The school performed the Mikado, and every year we had intelligence tests.

The poems I remember from school were the poet, Thomas Gray 1716-71 and his famous poem, 'Elegy written in a Country Churchyard'- set in the churchyard at Stoke Poges, starting with the words, 'The curfew tolls the knell of parting day" The books, Silas Marner, and Shakespeare's, 'The Merchant of Venice' and' Much To Do About Nothing.' When the Parliament had the Election after the war, we had to vote at school for a party, and I can remember my Father being so cross because that I had voted for Clement Attlee and not Winston Churchill, only because the boy who played Clement Attlee was the better speaker. Winston Churchill lost the election in Parliament much to my Father's disgust.

I loved all the gym and sports lessons, I was in the second Rounder and Hockey Teams and enjoyed playing the different schools of Roundhay, Wakefield, Thoresby and Cockburn. I attended different subjects to Dorothy and sat the School Certificate at fourteen. To pass the School Certificate you had to get five passes, a credit and a Distinction. My sister Dorothy passed it, with excellent results and was able to train to be an R.G.N. Nurse at Leeds General Infirmary. I sat the school certificate twice, the second time they said I was not old enough, and again I went down into the class below until I decided to leave school.

*Bob and Betty*

Shirley started Rothwell too in 1948 when she left Shirley worked for E.J Arnold, then Bovril and Heinz Company in the offices and went to night school for typing.

I caught the Scarlet Fever when I was thirteen in1948, the doctor decided that I did not need to go to hospital, I could stay at home in the bedroom reached through the bathroom. Only my mother was allowed to come into the bedroom. It was very hard for her and she always looked very tired. I became very close to my Mother at that time. For six weeks I had to stay in quarantine. I divided my time into sections, did jigsaws, I read the piles of magazines that my mother's friend brought me, and enjoyed especially the serials. The magazines of the early fifties were full of information and advice. I could not read any thick books because of infection. The magazines had to be burnt. One of the magazines was The Woman's Weekly that I still enjoy reading now. I was lucky to have a wireless too. I said it was like being in prison. The family all came into the bathroom next-door and shouted hello but no one could come in. Dorothy was so cross, because she had to have another two weeks off school too. Dorothy played on the piano for hours and the piano echoed around the house and was lovely to listen to.

In the last two weeks Shirley my sister who was younger than me started to play tennis with me through the window and down into the farmyard, I was so grateful she has had a place in my heart ever since. After four weeks the doctor decided that I could climb out of the bedroom window, onto the roof and down the ladder, and into the fields, as long as I stayed away from everyone. It was sheer bliss I had gone into that bedroom in the winter, and came out to the most beautiful spring. I do not think I had noticed nature before, the hedgerows and fields were a mass of flowers and the weather was warm and sunny. I loved to watch the swallows in the farmyard dive-bombing the cats and sometimes the outcome was sad and the cats got them

I became very close to my mam and noticed how pale and tired she was. I did my best to help her all I could after that. We found out later she had had a heart murmur since we were born.

I was confirmed in the St John's Church next to Lewis's in Leeds a month after, because I had missed the confirmation with my friends. My mother took me to Leeds and I came home with a red dress and because my mother liked me in both, a beautiful white one too, for the confirmation, my father was cross, because we had bought two dresses.

On the first day of term at school each pupil must bring a certificate on a prescribed form, signed by the parent, that there has been no contact with any infectious or contagious disease during this holiday. When such contact has been made, a medical certificate must be brought signed by a doctor, stating that the child was in fit condition to return to school my sister Dorothy had to take one in September 6th 1948. There were many children who caught Scarlet Fever and taken to the isolation hospitals at Garforth Cliff and Seacroft. One of my friends was in Seacroft Hospital for a year because she had caught other infections too.

*Harvest time*

# Chapter Six
# The Rothwell Grammar
# School summer camps

At Rothwell Grammar School there was school camp every year. I went to Kettleness, near Whitby, in 1947 with my sister Dorothy. We could have as much jam and bread, as we wanted if we were hungry. We were in tents of about six and had smaller toilet tents, in a farmer's field. The ride there was over the moors from Pickering to Whitby, and it was very foggy, when we passed The Hole Of Horcum it was a bit frightening, as we did not know how far away the edge was. The Heather was a deep purple and the moors when the fog lifted a marvellous sight. We walked over the cliffs to Runswick Bay, and enjoyed the lovely train ride down the coast to Whitby, (later axed by the Dr Beeching.) We washed in large troughs with the insect 'Boatman' swimming around.

In 1948 I went with Dorothy again to the school camp at Marske near Saltburn. This was a camp next to the seaside, we loved to go down the steep slope to Saltburn, my father and mother visited us there and took the only family photo we had taken. It was a lovely old coastal town with a long pier. We also visited Redcar.

In 1949 I went to Ingleton School camp with Shirley she had passed the eleven-plus and started Rothwell Grammar School too. We had to carry our heavy cases up the waterfalls with dire warnings that a child had drowned the previous week. We loved the open fields at Beazley Farm, washing our plates in the stream and walked into Ingleton and visited White Scar Caves and had lovely scones there. We walked up Ingleborough

Mountain and could see Morecambe Bay. We particularly enjoyed washing in the stream, and walking down the spectacular waterfalls to Ingleton. We found a swimming pool, it was icy cold, but we enjoyed it. When dusk fell the teachers joined us for hearty singsongs around the campfire, on the last night with large mugs of cocoa. We climbed the rocks and the white cliffs and seemed to have a lot of freedom.

A visit to Stratford Upon Avon with the school camp in 1950 was so much more interesting after the Architecture lessons. We went to the Stratford Memorial Theatre, in its beautiful position at the side of the river, to see the famous actor John Geilgud in Julius Caesar and Much Ado About Nothing. I was thrilled to hear the words spoken in such a rhythmical fashion. It was magical standing on the balcony overlooking the river Avon in the interval of the plays. We walked along the riverside to Anne Hathaway's Cottage. The New House had structured gardens, we looked round

*Farmyard 1947 Mount Pleasant Farm*

Shakespeare's House and the grounds were a mass of flowers. It was a working school camp and we had to write about Shakespeare and the History we had gained through the visits to Shakespeare's town of Stratford Upon Avon. I thought it was a beautiful place. The roads to the campsite were lined with Laburnum bushes. We so enjoyed those school holidays; because of the farm my father could not leave it to go on holiday. We got a rapturous welcome from the dogs when we came home and my mother and father so pleased to see us.

# Chapter seven
# Girls Friendly Society

The Girl's Friendly Society was held on a Monday night in the Rectory room situated in the right hand side of the 200-year-old Vicarage at Swillington. We looked forward to it. We went with Margaret Barraclough, a very dear friend whom I've known since she was three year old, when her brother George brought her to the farm. She always came to the same bus stop; at the top of Whitehouse Lane, we used to shout coo-ee to each other, to go to school and church. We had lovely rides in her uncle's pony and trap singing a rendition of 'Shine on harvest moon' and 'She'll be coming round the mountain'. They were everyone's favourite songs at that period. We used to play in a shed in the garden, when we were children amongst the chickens. At the side of it stood her uncle's polished and shiny pony and trap we enjoyed her company as she went to school, Sunday school and the G.F.S. with us. Margaret went to Roundhay High School and we went to Rothwell Grammar School and we did not see so much of her then, but when I worked in Leeds, I travelled on the bus every morning with her.

The Rectory windows looked onto a well tended large green lawn and gardens. There was an orchard behind the vicarage laden with russet apples in autumn. The winding driveway lined with multicoloured rhododendrons in spring. The Girl's Friendly Society was for eight-year-old to sixteen-year-old girls upwards and was very popular in all the churches in Leeds. Miss Howe and Mrs. Gummerson were in charge. Miss Howe had a sister who was the midwife in Swillington for many years and lived at Little Preston. Miss Metcalfe was the school nurse. We said prayers at the beginning and the end. We played

46

*back row: friend, friend Dorothy, Aunt Nellie, Dad*
*front row: friend Shirley, Thomas, Betty, Mam*

*Dorothy's 60th Birthday*

47

lots of games, and learnt Country Dances in which we displayed at the Garden Fete in the summer. First Aid was taught to us, too. We had meetings and competitions with other churches in Leeds. I can remember going to The Venerable Bede Church in Leeds on Armley Road. We entered a play in a competition we had written from Little Women. I can still remember the lines spoken by Jo in the first few lines, [Christmas won't be Christmas without any presents] because Marmee, their Mother in the story, had given the presents, with their permission to a poor family. We also performed a play from Alice in Wonderland, the Mad Hatters Tea Party. My sister Dorothy, played the part of the Mad Hatter and my sister Shirley, played the sleepy Dormouse, amid much laughter, as she had to be put in the teapot in the end.

We had some interesting days out, taking buses from Leeds Town Hall to Keighley, and then on to Haworth, We had sandwiches in the large park, before walking up the cobbled streets to Haworth Parsonage and church. As schoolchildren we were steeped in the history of the Bronte sisters and loved to read all about them and their life at Haworth, and thought it was so interesting in the museum. It made us sad to see the gravestones in the churchyard, to see how young the Bronte sisters were when they died. After looking round the church we set off on the footpath to the moors. I cannot remember it raining on these visits to the waterfall, and across the little bridge, and over the other side to Top Withins, featured in Emily Bronte's book (1818-1848) 'Wuthering Heights.' We followed the stony path over the purple heather clad moors, leading past the reservoir and back to Haworth, and the long journey, home by bus. We had seen the films of 'Wuthering Heights' and 'Jane Eyre' written by Charlotte Bronte (1816-1855) and read the books too and we were so thrilled to be there. Anne Bronte (1820-1849) who wrote 'The Tenant of

Wildfell Hall' is buried at Scarborough.

I was still going to the G. F.S. when I was fifteen; A missionary, Miss Kind visited and showed us slides all about a school in India, that we had a collection for each week India seemed a magical place. In 1951 we entered competitions at Allerton High School and made raffia baskets. On the 17th June we attended a huge service at Ripon Cathedral. My mother came too, and especially enjoyed it, when my sister Shirley carried the G.F. S. Banner up the aisle, with so many other groups of the G. F. S. all around Yorkshire. We also had special days at Ilkley walking up to the Whitehouse and across the moors to the Cow and Calf rocks.

We practiced for The Church Garden Fete, which featured the G.F. S. in so many activities. We manned the stalls; I noted that Derreen and I had made seven pounds on the pop stall, on the 18th June, and that there were men gymnasts giving displays, Stalls with penny rolling boards our favourite was the hoop-la stall. We did displays of Country Dancing accompanied to an old wind up gramophone. There was a G.F.S. Pageant in the Royal Albert Hall when Queen Mary attended, in the early 1900's. The G.F.S. is still continuing in Blackburn in Lancashire.

Our lives revolved around the church, of St Mary's at Swillington and the support from the vicars of Swillington. Mr. Cranmer and Mr.Gillot and all the people who made our lives extra special including Miss Howe, Mrs. Gummerson, Mrs. Noble and Mrs. Oubridge We really looked forward to the Monday nights and the outings in the school holidays.

# Chapter eight
# Teenage Years

My friend Derreen came to live at WellGreen farm at Garforth Bridge on June 15th 1941 when she was six year old; my father had taken over shortly before, renting it from Mr Dawson. The farm was set in beautiful countryside and there was a pathway to Brecks Farm, which led through a wood filled with bluebells in spring. The hedgerow leading down to Garforth Bridge sheltered the peeping violets, which we looked for every spring. Foster Darley lived in the farmhouse first, and Derreen's family lived in the house next door. Foster Darley then moved down Brecks Lane Farm and Derreen moved into the farmhouse. Well Green Farm is now demolished and the Hilton Hotel in its place at Garforth Bridge. Derreen's father, Dick Linley was the manager at Mount Pleasant Farm and won lots of prizes for ploughing. He was a very pleasant smiling man. He had worked at Carters' Farm at Seacroft before moving to Garforth Bridge.

Derreen and I went on holiday together and to the pictures. I spent many hours at Well Green Farm, her Mother always had time to sit and talk to us in front of the huge coal fire. Derreen and I loved to dress up and dance in the fields. We played in the haystacks, and enjoyed cricket, playing with her brother Derek, who later helped my dad on the farm. We went to town on a Saturday afternoon; we had such happy times there, looking round the shops and Leeds Market. I would buy material for my dressmaking class in Swillington; my father bought me a new Jones sewing machine instead of the old treadle machine. There was a haystack fire in those childhood years, at Well Green Farm, my Father said the cause was spontaneous combustion, and loss of the haystack cost him a lot of money.

Derreen after leaving Castleford Grammar School worked at the Naylor and Pollard Pilot Works at Garforth Bridge making cotton overalls and shirts. The Pilot Works had a holiday scheme where we paid 2/6d a week for a year, to save for a week's holiday to go to Scarborough. We climbed to the

*Betty and Shirley*

*Betty Dorothy and Shirley*

51

castle and sat listening to Hoagy Carmichael's, 'My Resistance is Low.' playing at the amusement park nearby. We caught the boat, either the Yorkshire Lady or Coronia out of the harbour every day and were delighted if the sea was rough. We ran down the gardens in Peasholm Park, we were staying in one of the streets at the top of the gardens. We had beautiful carefree days together, such a sweet tempered friend, we never had a cross word. We had some lovely times. We caught the train to Bridlington and Scarborough, for the day costing 50p, and even paid £1-50p, for the whole week, going every day from Garforth Station to Bridlington, Scarborough and Whitby. We loved to play Frankie Laine's record Jezebel on the Juke box in the amusements, and sat on the sands, we went roller skating in a hall near the Grand Hotel.

Garforth had a feast every summer at the top of the main Street, filled with shows, and a motorbikes going around The Wall of Death. Waltzers too, fast cars going round and round, A tightrope dancer, in the little circus, and plenty of stalls to roll pennies down and the chance to win a goldfish.

We scoured the Skyrack the local paper, when it came and decided which pictures we wanted to see that week, it must have been reasonably priced as we went three times in the week. Garforth Picture House had a matinee on a Saturday afternoon; the bus from Swillington was packed with noisy children. There was always a serial on first, usually a cowboy where all the children shouted for the hero, followed by a B. rated film and then the big picture. The first picture I remember seeing there was Errol Flynn in 'San Antonio' a film they are still showing now on T.V. The Shaftesbury, at Harehills was a popular place, The Ritz opened in 1920 and Regal opened in 1936 in Crossgates and with the Garforth Picture house were very popular picture houses they were always packed. It was an ideal place for teenagers to meet. The Regal was a more luxurious place with a balcony; we saw pictures like The Robe there. I think the ticket prices were higher. In Leeds we saw Gone With The Wind and The Great Caruso. Our favourite films starred Jane Powell and Doris Day, with excellent dancing and singing.

Further down Wakefield Road was Blackwells, consisting of two cottages, with a lovely oak tree with a seat round it, our friends the Darleys' and Dickensons lived there. Barbara Darley we still see now at Whist drives. A footpath ran past these cottages to Little Preston where another friend Margaret lived. We had some very happy times chatting outside her house as teenagers, with our friends who arrived back from Whitwood Technical College.

In 1951, I joined the Garforth Dramatic Society and played

*Mount Pleasant Farm, Swillington*

the maid in 'When We Were married' but because I had such a Yorkshire accent I started Elocution lessons with a lady in Detroit Avenue.

When I was seventeen I made friends with Sheila who worked with Keith, Shirley's future husband at the Copperworks in Leeds. The four of us had some lovely bike rides on a Saturday. We rode to Knaresborough along the riverside and had some very welcome pint pots of tea at the café, set in a garden near the river. We rowed on the river and called at Mother Shipton's Wishing Well. We cycled to York to the York Minster, walked round the walls, and visited the Castle Museum and the shops in the Shambles. Our bikes must have been safe to leave. We took our sandwiches and drinks. It wasn't an expensive day out. There was a special café in Otley where cyclists gathered. Shirley and I have always been close and good friends all our lives and always had lots of fun together.

Bob [my husband of 45 yrs.] went to school at Colton and

*Dorothy Mother Tom and Shirley*

Osmondthorpe High School until he was fifteen years old. He had mended radios, making one of his own, from being quite small. A teacher noting this gift got him the job at Stampers, a Radio and Television shop on Station Road Crossgates. He worked there straight from school and had forty-three years of working for that shop, as a Radio and Television engineer. Hirst and Symmonds owned the shop, latterly bought by Mr. Castle

Bob had had a heart murmur as a child and was not allowed to do games at school or be accepted into the army for National Service. Needless to say he was an excellent runner and seemed very fit. When he was three year old he got badly burned when his pyjamas caught fire. He was in Seacroft Hospital for a year because he caught Chicken Pox too. Bob had a shed in the garden that he had his radios and electricity equipment in. He has always been so good, all our married life at mending and repairing everything to do with the house garden and cars. I have been very fortunate to have a husband that can do repairs, and envied for it. Bob has always been ready to help anyone, a well-loved and respected gentleman.

I met Bob in the Welfare Hall Swillington at one of the dances they held every Friday night; he had a motorbike, a great attraction to me. Bob was only sixteen and I was seventeen. Bob was with his friend Michael and they split my friend and I to dance with us. I was keen on dancing and Bob was a good dancer, especially the Quick Step, one of my favourites, we also danced the Waltz, Harry Lime Theme, Valeta, and the Military Two Step. Tom Noble and his Band played the music, he was the organist at Swillington Church. On a Monday with his wife Mary, he gave dancing lessons at Colton Institute. On a Saturday he played down Carter Terrace Hollyshaw Lane Whitkirk Our favourite music at that time was Tihuana Brass, Swedish Rhapsody and Mr Sandman. We had some lovely times with a very good crowd of young people. We went on a bus with Tom Noble who was playing at the Riley Smith Hall (Bob supplied the amplifier for Tom Noble) at Tadcaster. I had been to quite a few dances with Bob, when I decided that Bob was nicer than any other boy I had met. We have been together now for fifty years. My Mother and Dad thought the world of him and Keith, Shirley's boyfriend then.

We went to several dances that Christmas and on New Year's Eve we went to the Golf House at Templenewsam, a very posh affair with long dresses on some of the ladies, We wore ankle length black taffeta skirts and white blouses. There was a buffet there and at the Riley Smith Hall.

Bob asked if I wanted to go to Scarborough on the bike the next day. I remember it being very frosty but what a sight coming into Scarborough under the Valley Bridge. It was first of many such rides on that motorbike, to see so many glorious sunsets, that followed some marvellous hot weather in 1952. There were some tremendous traffic jams on the roads to the coast because of the good weather, with no York bypass built then, and partly because of the railway gates across the roads, especially at Malton, Whitby and Scarborough.

We went to Whitby to Sandsend; we enjoyed the Magpie Café there. In Scarborough we parked on Scalby Mills and walked over the cliffs. How we loved to ride on that front, and have a dinner at the Welcome Inn, or Bamfords fish and chips. We went dancing to the Spa Ballroom and the Corner café and spent a lot of time in Peasholm Park. Bob has always taken great care of me since we were very young teenagers.

When I first met Bob I was helping in Swillington Church in 1953 to produce a Nativity play, and we asked if he could arrange the music in the church. The procession of the nativity wound round the edge of the church to the sound of the Hallelujah chorus from Handel's Messiah. It was quite effective and we got lots of compliments.

My friend Mary had a television set and we watched 'What's My Line' and 'Come Dancing' with Victor Sylvester and his Orchestra. He showed a new dance every week, it was very strict tempo, with Quicksteps and Waltzes. It was so lovely to watch as they were all in suits and floaty dresses. We went to the dances at the Capitol, Astoria and Majestic Ballrooms with large live bands. I remember watching the Queen's Coronation on June 1953 on Television at the school in Swillington on a rainy day, and going to the pictures to see it in colour.

# Chapter Nine
# Leeds Children's Day

My Mother's sister, Nellie lived on Street Lane, it was very convenient to Roundhay Park, it consisted of the Mansion House, over 600 acres of landscaped park with a large natural arena, two lakes, a maze, and bandstand. The highlight of the summer was Children's Day held every year. We caught the bus to Whitkirk church and then the number 38 bus to Oakwood Clock and the tram to Roundhay Park. We sat on Hill 60 to get the best view. My cousin Audrey was one of the attendants one year. I remember her pretty dress hanging up in the bedroom. What a spectacle to watch with thousands of children from all the schools in Leeds, making patterns on the huge arena, with Country Dancing, Gymnasts and races. Maypole dancing with all the pretty ribbons dancing in the wind, as the children weaved in and out. In the park were donkey rides, the steamer on the big Lake, and the paddleboats on the smaller Lake, a fairground, and an open-air theatre with children's shows.

Elsie Morrell Baxter helped to promote Children's Day in Leeds, as she was worried about the children of Leeds and their health, and thought the training would be good for them. She also introduced National Savings in schools too. The Queen of Children's day was chosen from all the schools in Leeds, after reciting a poem. Her attendants were chosen from the same school. The outfits paid for by the Y. E. P. and Schofields designed and made them. They were very pretty and special.

On Children's Day the Queen and her attendants would set

off from the Town Hall Leeds with the Lord Mayor, a huge procession, to finally parade around the arena. I remember Queen Elizabeth came, before she was queen, to a very warm welcome. I can't remember it raining. In 1946 over 90,000 people attended, there were special trams to take the people to the park. We loved to go to the open-air swimming pool there, and the canal gardens, which were a riot of colour in the summer and it was fun to feed the ducks.

# Chapter Ten
# Wartime

My dad's brother's son William died in the war at Calvados in France on the 4<sup>th</sup> August 1944, I remember the sadness in the family.

Call-up to War started on August 1939 for 18 year old to 36-year old. Blackout started in 3rd September 1939, no visible lights between sunset and sunrise. 1940 Emergency Power Act empowered the Ministry of Labour, to exercise complete control of manpower to decide the job of every adult, age fourteen to sixty-five years, including the unfit. Ernest Bevin ordered that all men had to find a job or join up. There was a million unemployed in 1940 in Britain and in 1943 there was full employment of 22 million. By June 1944 almost a third of the male population of working age were in the services.

Most men in Agriculture were classed as reservists. I remember my Father and Mother listening to the news on the wireless with grave faces. There were 600,000 farm workers before the War, their minimum wage were forty-seven shillings. 6.5 per cent of British Homes were destroyed in air attacks. America sent food under the Lend Lease; this meant we had not to pay for it until after the war, including tins of salmon and spam.

Agriculture before the outbreak of war in 1939 it was run down, badly administered industry, neglected by the governments between the wars. It was a victim of worldwide slumps, imports of cheap food fruit, cereals and timber and animal feed. The farmers and farm workers were depressed, wages and living standards were at low ebb. Stock had very

*Shirley and Keith's Wedding*

*Bob Betty and Grand children*

61

few pure breeds; Poor yields were accompanied by poor prices paid. Farmers had to change to a self-producing highly intensive crop management to increase yields and improve stock output. The first stage of change was at government level. It had to give priority to parts of the industry, i.e. wheat barley oats bread, feeding stuffs for both human and animals. It was decided that the Ministry of Agriculture and Fisheries should set up County Agricultural and Executive Committees, [CAEC's]. The National Farmers Union, County Landowners' Association, and Agricultural Workers' Union were all involved at the start of the war in local Agricultural Executive Committees. [AEC's]. There were County Liaison Officers who liased from the county commissioners down to the local committees. These had very wide powers. They gave directions to farmers and landowners on the cultivation and management of the land. The main aim was to see that the country fulfilled its quota of land to be ploughed, in order to increase the acreage of the main crops.

The children were allowed time off to work on the land, the October break was always called the potato picking holiday, children came to pick the potatoes on the farm. The older boys helping with the harvest. The farm was busy with plenty to do. We had fifteen men at one time working on the two farms. My mother made butter, sitting in the backfield for hours, turning the heavy wooden churn until the cream separated from the rich milk, and turned to butter which was in great demand We had to queue up for ration books at the Welfare Hall at Swillington. The clocks were turned forward two hours to make double summertime in the war years. The summers were hot and the storms were quite severe. I remember my Father covering the dressing table mirror because of the lightning. In 1942 the Ministry of War had the top of Whitehouse Lane for a Polish camp, and they came for eggs.

Apart from one night when bombs were dropped in the field nearby, I remember crawling into my mother's bed and listening to my heart bounding, I cannot think the war came near us.

We had two evacuees who attended Swillington school from Kent, who were relatives of Myers, our friends who lived at Quality Court in Swillington. Dorothy went down to the Festival of Britain in 1951 and on to Kent with their family after the war. Our Land Girls were, Jennie Gill from Huddersfield, and Lily Saville from Outgang farm Heslington York. I went home with Lily and they had large photos of soldiers who had been in the First World War.

The Land Girls in the war wore corduroy breeches in brown/beige colour, and leggings and boots, dark green jumpers, brown jacket and khaki brown hats. The Land Girls had seven paid days holiday a year and every six weeks, a travel pass home. They had four weeks training and minimum wage was thirty-five shillings and nine pence, maximum deduction for board was sixteen shillings and six pence, overtime was ten pence an hour. In 1941 there were 20,000 women in the Land Army and in 1944 there were 80,000 working on the land. Elsie helped my mother in the house who had replaced Hilda, who had been with us from babies. Hilda joined up in the services for the duration of the war and came back to the farm, but left again when I finished school and worked at home. Elsie took me to Castleford Feast, I remember the Shamrock, a huge big swing and we missed the last bus home and my Father had to pay for a Taxi and was not pleased, Elsie used to bleached coif in the front of her hair.

Nutritionist, Elsie Widdowson 1906-2,000, CH. CBE. FRC at the Imperial College London formulated the rations 8oz sugar, 2oz of tea, 8oz of meat, 2oz of cheese, 2oz of butter, 4oz margarine. 2oz of lard, one egg every two weeks, one packet of dried egg every four-weeks, two half pints of milk, 4oz of bacon or ham, 12oz of sweets every four weeks. It was said that the people had never been healthier. Everybody had an Identity card and a Ration Book, which we obtained, from the Welfare Hall Swillington, with a page of coupons for various commodities, meat, bacon, sugar, butter, and cheese.

Keith told me that his mother paid the doctor in the village a small amount each week before the national Health Service was set up, the doctor informed if she paid him a pound they would be straight. She said she had no idea how much she owed him really, it could have said £100 and she would have been no wiser.

# Chapter Eleven
# Swillington Church Social Life

There was a church at Swillington in 1886, a church in the Manor of Kippax and Ledston. St Mary's church is situated on the main Aberford to Wakefield Road seven miles east of Leeds. It is six miles to Aberford and seven to Wakefield. The Wakefield road was made between 1775 and 1800. The records of the church can be traced back to 1291. The church was demolished in the 14 century, and rebuilt and the present nave, aisles and chancel dates from this rebuilding, using creamy yellow magnesium limestone. The tower was built mid 15th century and was refaced 1884 by Mr. Chorley of Leeds Sandstone came from the quarry at Harehills and has blackened with atmospheric pollution over the years. The nave floor was flagged. The altar in the sanctuary was dedicated to All Hallows and the vestry was rebuilt in 1880. The Parish Register from 1539 is one of the oldest in the country. There is a three-sided altar rail with kneeling mats in the middle of 19th century. The altar in the sanctuary was dedicated to All Hallows. The north side has the Chapel of Our Lady.

In 1902 a new oak roof was placed on the chancel, donated by Mary Lowther of Swillington House. On the south side is the Chapel of St Nicholas which was occupied by the Lowther family who were the Lords of the manor. They lived at Swillington House, which overlooked the River Aire surrounded by beautiful parkland, which included many rare trees; The Lowthers moved to Swillington in 1663-1920 and were great benefactors of the Church and village. They provided money to build schools and almshouses, and maintained the church and developed the local collieries. The family of Lowther are buried in Swillington Church.

Sir William Lowther 1694-1763 rebuilt Swillington House in 1804 and its stables for 4,000 pounds. He was an M.P and was extremely studious he had a large library and was a man of extensive learning and knowledge. The Lowther's had thirty horses in their stable, which provided work for the Blacksmith who lived in the Blacksmiths Cottage on Jinny Moor Lane. It had a large icehouse in the grounds; the estate consisted of 2,000 acres. The Lowthers had 20 indoor servants, 14 gardeners and numerous estate workers. The park was stocked with rare trees brought by the Lowther family from all over the world.

In 1919 the Lowthers sold the contents of Swillington Hall and the valuable 'Zouch' library of books, many antiques were included in the sale some of them in Harewood House now. Sir Charles Hugh Lowther 1803-94, their descendant, was a well-known, very clever person although he was blind. When he was fourteen his mother acquired some books from France, printed in an embossed italic type, with which he learnt to read. In 1822 he obtained a French Printing press and Charles was able to produce books for his own use, including the Gospels and Epistles and became the first reader and embosser of books for the blind in Britain. Dr. William Moon developed a special type. It was based on simplified Capital letters of Embossed dots. Braille was not introduced in the U.K. until 1869. Charles Lowther became a great supporter of Dr Moon. He provided at his own expense, 21,00 Bibles and other books in Moon's embossed type to Libraries. Charles was extremely well informed; his wife Isabella read to him the literatures and general intelligence of the day. He took a great interest in social problems. He lived to 91 years

In 1902 when George Lowther [1837-90], Charles Lowther's eldest son died, his widow Mary Alice {Bingham], after the First World War gave the beautiful stained glass east window of the chancel, representing the Messiah, the Patriarchs Isaac, led by an angel, and Jacob his son Joseph with scriptural texts, in memory of her father in law Sir Charles Lowther who died in 1894 and her husband George Lowther who died in France and is buried in Swillington church.

Mary Francis Lowther also gave the east window of the south aisle representing Christ, the King of Peace, gave in thanksgiving for Victory and Peace after the Great War, as a Lowther family memorial to the church for the safe return of her two sons and son-in law, and to the war work done by her two daughters who had received the M.B.E.

In 1920 they sold the Swillington Hall to the Bower's Family who owned the mines. The Bower's family sold Swillington House again in 1935 including twelve farms, Little Preston Hall and 100 cottages. Charles Davies from Ledston bought most of the land and built the houses around Church Avenue. Swillington village was primarily farming with the development of outcropping and deep mining in the early 1900's. Pease and Partners bought out T. and R. Bowers Primrose Pit, the mining shaft was situated at Mount Pleasant pit that closed in 1970 and the area turned into a picnic place.

The Hall was demolished in 1950's because of the mining subsidence, and the stables made into a private home. The north Lodge once guarded the entrance of the Park and Home Farm, through a lime avenue and cricket pitch. Adjoining the St Mary's Church on Church Lane is the Old School and School House and was one of the four schools within the district, Swillington Parochial School, The Mount Private School on Swillington Lane where the Lowthers and their friends attended, and Bowers Allerton School on Astley Lane.

Swillington St Mary's was a beautiful comfortable old church the atmosphere was so friendly. We were a good crowd of teenagers that attended the church services on Sundays,

10am and 6pm and the Sunday school was at 2 0'clock. Christmas Easter and Whitsuntide were special times. The first organ in the church cost £69 donated by Richard Green in early 1800's and a new one in 1887 donated by F. Leather Esquire from Leventhorpe Hall and built by Hill and Son. In the 1940's the organist was Tom Noble from Colton he always played well-known and seasonal hymns He was the organist for over forty years. The choir was very good, and included Tom Noble's brother, Fred Noble a very accomplished singer.

The church tower contains two sets of bells, with the original set dating from 1656 and 1732. I helped to ring the Church Bells too, nearly reached the roof when I hung on to the rope too long but managed to let go in time. It was a bit scary up the narrow steps to the belfry tower, but a lovely view from the top over Swillington. The Church Bells were rung for our wedding in 1957. Mr Guy Cox and friends replaced the Bells because the structure was not safe An eight set of bells came from St Matthew's Church Holbeck being cast in the 1800's, and dedicated at Swillington in 1978 and now played again in their full glory.

A path ran from the Rectory to Saint Mary's Church Swillington, called The Lady's Walk, a very pretty way, the path consisting of sculptured stones from the old tower of the church, to form a border along by the gravestones, through the little gate, and passed the lawns of the Rectory. We loved the statue of the Angel in the churchyard. The vicars that were at Saint Mary church when we attended were Reverend Buck, The Reverend Cranmer, The Reverend Gillott and The Reverend Rayner who married Bob and me in 1957. The Reverend Burgheim was a famous Vicar of Swillington who was the model for Holman Hunt's Painting 'The Light Of The World' in the 1800's.

The Harvest Festival was a lovely time in church all the

*Betty and Shirley*

*Derreen and Betty*

*Thomas*

windowsills and corners filled with fragrant apples and flowers. The font surrounded by the fruits of the harvest and a loaf of bread shaped as a sheaf of corn. 'We Plough The Fields and Scatter The Good Seed on The Land' was sung with gusto, as many of the congregation was farmers. It was a very friendly community there were lots of miners who worked at Mount Pleasant Pit and Allerton Bywater Pit that attended the church. On Easter Sunday, the hymns played were always the old familiar sounds only sung on that day, I especially liked 'Jesus Christ is Risen Today'. The church was well attended. There was only a boy's choir who sat altogether near the altar in their white surplices; The choirboys had a girlfriend who sat altogether at the bottom of the church, but there were some beautiful voices amongst the girls. Dorothy and Margaret sang in of the Leeds Philharmonic Society Choir. When the service ended we would all congregate at the church gate. After talking there for half an hour, about eight of them would accompany me up Betty Log Hill, around Whitehouse Lane and back down Wakefield Road leaving me at the farm.

We had Sunday school picnics and games at Miss Nichols' Farm in the summer, which we could see from the bedroom window of the farm. The church had a very good Sunday school; I was a Sunday school teacher, with my friend Margaret. It was lovely to enter the church to the sound of children all waiting to greet you, ready to sing all the special children's hymns, then to divide around the church to have the bible stories read to them. My class used the pews near a wooden effigy, set in a case in the 14th century tomb recess in the south aisle which had an ogee arch with mouldings, including a line of small square flowers also seen on the tower arches.

We had a Sunday School Christmas Party in the little school, with the screen pushed back, over fifty children came and had a lovely time playing team games and a tea party We had a Sunday school outing to Bridlington every summer, although I was nine before I saw the sea, the war prevented us going before. On a Sunday school outing to Bridlington, we had had such a lovely time running in and out of the sea, but we got sunburnt especially my sister Dorothy, who that night when we came home had such a large blister on her back, when we poured the bath water over it, it filled up like a balloon. Needless to say she avoided the sun after that as she had bright ginger hair and a very fair skin. We took a bus to Flamborough where my mother had spent her holidays as a teenager. I am sure the parents of the children who were at Sunday school thoroughly enjoyed the peace and quiet at home on a Sunday afternoon

Christmas too was a magical time with the church windowsills all decorated, a huge Christmas tree near the altar.

The font is an octagonal cup shaped bowl, the sides tapering with the base and stems. It is lead lined. The movable oak cover consists of octagonal lid moulded on the edge, which bears eight radiating trusses rising from the angles and meeting in a central balustrade. The font may have been made in the 17th century and was beautifully decorated with a Nativity scene.

*Dorothy R.G.N*

The beautiful hymns of Christmas time sung in Church. The choir sang around Swillington village on Christmas Eve. I remember one magical Christmas Eve when the snow started falling as we reached home at twelve o'clock. A time for Christmas parties held in the homes of our friends. We can all claim to over forty years of marriage, perhaps because we had such a good Christian start.

We could walk all the footpaths and leafy lanes of Swillington without concern, although my father always set the time for us to be back home, usually before ten o'clock, unless there was a dance. I used to bicycle home at twelve o'clock from the dances at Swillington, believing it to be safe.

I went to church three times on a Sunday, G.F. S. on a Monday and Youth club on a Friday in the 200-year-old rectory. It was a very busy place with Church meetings in 1945-1951, held there in a room on the left hand side, it had an open fire and a fireguard which made it very cosy in winter. The Youth Club was open on a Sunday and Friday night and we played table tennis and quiz nights. Sometimes with a visiting team from Kippax or Garforth Youth Club, we enjoyed a very good social life with some very good friends. Unfortunately the boys all had to join up at eighteen, and go into the Army, Navy and Air Force to serve their National Service. Our friendship is still strong to this day, but we went our separate ways and met and married other people.

# Chapter Twelve
# Harvest time

After the harvest the huge Marshall's threshing machine came, a huge monstrosity, puffing smoke out, replaced with the combine harvester now. What a sight that thresher was, puffing smoke out it filled the driveway, causing great excitement, Everyone coming to watch it as it made its way to the stackyard, where it stayed for at least two days.   What a dusty job it was, with the straw separating from the chaff from the wheat. It was unhealthy work, the dust penetrated into the nose and eyes of the men. Extra men coming to help, including my uncle Den and cousin Dennis. The dogs running excitedly barking and catching the rats especially when the stack got lower. The men were frightened of the rats as they said the rats would jump up to their throats, the mice ran up their trouser legs, if they hadn't got them tied up with string

My mother always gave the men from the Thrasher machine, a substantial dinner at twelve o'clock and 'drinkings' the name we gave to the huge mugs of tea, scones sandwiches at harvest time morning and afternoon. There were fifteen men at times working on the Harvest. There was satisfaction when the harvest was safely in.

After the golden corn was all safely away in the granary at the bottom of the yard Mr. Newman the corn merchant came to buy the corn. (A bill shows J Dawson seed merchants bought 76 cwts. of wheat for £17-8s-4d.) Today with the aid of combine harvesters something my father never had, corn is cut and threshed in one operation, and no-one regrets the passing of the threshing machine The farm workers are well rid of the dirty dusty job and the hard work involved.

My father grew a variety of crops sown on a rota basis, including wheat, barley, oats, clover, turnips, mangolds and potatoes. The crops were rotated in the fields. The wheat barley oats were cash crops, and the turnips and mangolds were chopped in the turnip chopper and fed to the animals. Oats and barley were sown in February. Oats were animal feed for horses. The bedding for the cows was the straw left after the threshing machine sorted the wheat from the chaff.

Harvesting took at least a month, haymaking began in July, the grass was cut and left until the sap had dried, and the swathes were turned over with wooden rakes. It was left until the grass turned dark green colour and became the beautiful smelling hay. It was gathered into cocks, left to dry, and then it was forked onto an elevator that carried it on to a stack.

After the corn was cut with a binder, it was packed into sheaves and tied, the sheaves of corn were brought into the stackyard, it was made into a stack of a solid weatherproof unit, it was important if rainwater seeped into a stack the grain was effected and the value reduced. I remember my parents having a Harvest Party and a barrel of beer and food from Freemans at Garforth. We had bad harvests too when there was nothing to celebrate. One year my father had no money for presents at Christmas. My father worried about the cost of our school uniforms bought in Leeds at Rawcliffes. I remember Shirley knitting furiously to get a cardigan ready for school.

We attended the Farmers Union dinners that were held at the Guildford and Gilpin Hotels in Leeds. The Yorkshire Show at Harrogate was the highlight of the summer. The show jumping and the animals, the craft and flower tents it was a special day out.

In 1954 the placing of electricity in the farmhouse and buildings was a huge undertaking, my father had to agree to pay a minimum payment of £42 a year for five years. There was dust and dirt every where as the men drilled into the old walls to run the wires and put the plugs in, to clear up every day, when the workman finished, it was hard work to clean with a carpet sweeper and brush and shovel. At the same time a coal place outside the kitchen door was made into a toilet, a cesspool dug in the field for the waste. We no longer had to go up the garden path, to the old toilet with its two well-scrubbed wooden seats. I missed the view over the fields but not the emptying of the potties. It was lovely to go out of the kitchen to well lit rooms as it was a bit scary in winter, with only a candle to light your way.

Freedom when it was all finished, my mother had a Parnell washing machine instead of the boiler, Peggy tub and the heavy mangle. A Dryer was bought too, with the washing hung on rails in a square container, without having to use the creel over the fire, which made Mondays on a wet day so cold and damp. A vacuum cleaner instead of having to get down on hands and knees, and much more efficient than the carpet sweeper. The clipped rugs did not take kindly to the vacuum that pulled the loose clips out. We looked in amazement how much dust came out of the carpets. The electric iron was my favourite, an end to the heavy flat irons that cooled down so quickly. The housework and the washing and ironing were done so much quicker. My mother still preferred the coal fire and found the small electric cooker bought for seven pounds, nineteen and six pence, dried up her cakes and the pans boiled over because she could not regulate the heat. All these electrical appliances were bought from Stampers in Crossgates where my future husband worked.

To have electricity on the farm made such a difference, lights in the mistal for the men instead of the Tilley lamp, electric milking machines and coolers for the milk, potato sorters and Swede cutters. We kept the coal fire in the kitchen with its lovely fireguard that was lovely to sit on to warm your back.

One really sad event was the accident, when little Floss our dog, my constant companion, was killed by the electricity van [that had given us so much freedom) on the main road Floss had followed Thomas who was farming in the field, a thing she had never done before. What a sad sight that was, Thomas carrying the limp body of Floss up the drive. I was heartbroken, as were all the family.

Life in the farmhouse changed after we had electricity put in, the television was put in the far room with its electric fire, it divided the family who before, only sat round the kitchen table at night. Because my father did not like most of the programmes, he sat in solitude in his large wooden chair in the kitchen, in front of the black leaded fireplace listening to the wireless. Its funny but the farmhouse seemed a colder place somehow.

The programmes I remember on T.V. were the Queen's Coronation, Wooden Tops, What's My Line, and Victor Sylvester's Dance Programmes that was very strict tempo. The quicksteps and waltzes were lovely to watch, as the dancers wore special floaty dresses.

*Roland and Dorothy Marson's wedding*

*Samuel and Lucy Naylor's wedding*

*Catherine Osborn*
*Paternal Grandma*

*Catherine and*
*William Osborn*

# Chapter Thirteen
# Work at Home

At fifteen I left school and stayed at home to help my mother in the house and with the milk round my father had around the Killingbeck and Foundry Lane areas. A typical week's work in the house consisted of a set pattern of housework. Every day the rugs in the kitchen were taken up, the floor swept, and the sideboards dusted. The six-coal buckets filled from the coal tipped near the back door, and sticks to be chopped to light the kitchen fire. I used paraffin sometimes, but if too liberally given, I set the chimney on fire. The beds had to be made, every week the top sheet went to the bottom of the bed and a clean one on the top. Blankets of fine yellow wool were washed in summer.

Washday was a great event; on a Sunday the heavy soiled items such as the towels were soaked in soda in a large white bowl. On Monday morning it was an early start, with the lighting of the copper boiler in the washhouse next to the kitchen door. The whites boiled for about ten minutes, taken out with care, rinsed with dolly blue and starched, and put through the heavy mangle, a large wooden structure with an iron frame. The rest of the washing was possed in a large silver Peggy tub and again put through the heavy mangle. It took until to about two o'clock in the afternoon. On a nice drying day the washing was put on huge washing lines near the back door because we were on top of the hill it caught all the wind. But if it was raining it was put on the creel over the kitchen fire to dry. It was then damped and rolled up ready for ironing. The cats liked the warm washhouse and appeared from the barn to sleep near the copper boiler. The backrooms scrubbed or swept; on a Monday we had baked potatoes, cold meat and rice pudding.

The ironing took all day Tuesday, the heavy flat irons heated in the oven, I hated ironing because the iron always seemed to be too hot or too cold, a long tedious job. My mother and father usually went to Leeds Market in the afternoon, when we were little they bought colouring books from Stringers and bought loose biscuits, that were kept in large tins on the stalls. They brought the latest song sheet from the music shop in the arcade. Tuesday dinner was, liver, onions, and sausages.

Wednesday was the bedroom and the first and far rooms day, the floors dusted and swept, my favourite dinner of the week Wednesday, the bone from the meat to make stew, with plenty of vegetables, Yorkshire puddings and delicious oxo gravy.

Thursday was baking day, starting in the morning with the yeast, flour water and lard placed in a large yellow baking bowl in front of the fire to rise, kneaded after an hour and the left again and shaped again and put in loaf tins, and baked in the coal oven. My mother moving the coal in the fire near the oven, or away from it to reach the right temperature for whatever she was baking. There was no better taste than homemade bread and butter and homemade raspberry, blackberry and strawberry jam. After the bread had been baked the pastry followed, fruit pies, cakes buns custard pies fruitcakes, teacakes, and the special lemon curd tarts that my friend Margaret enjoyed. Everyone had something sweet to finish his or her lunches and teas for a week. The meat and fish delivered fresh, every week. We had chops for dinner on Thursday.

On a Sunday we had a special tea, my father's brother and his wife, aunt Dolly and uncle Glen came to tea, we had salmon or crab, jelly blancmange and cream. My mother bottled fruit and a lady came to show her how to bottle the very hard pears from the orchard. The apples from the orchard were picked in the autumn and kept down the cellar a cold damp place, to give us delicious apple pies every week, my mother always did the baking and took great pride in it. We ate margarine instead of butter, and saccharin's in our tea. The sugar ration was used for baking.

Friday was the kitchen and pantry, cleaning day, the stone floors scrubbed on hands and knees with large tablets of green soap. The large square kitchen table was scrubbed every Friday and the cool stone tops of the walk in pantry too, stored there, were jars of dripping, homemade jam and marmalade, the homemade bread was kept in a large pottery jar on the floor, and cakes and buns were all kept in tins on the top. Under the slabs were the pails of milk and the delicious cream on top. Also the eggs preserved in a bucket. We had to scrub the wooden tops of the toilet seat and the flagged floor in the toilet situated up the garden. The silver cutlery and cake stand polished. The order came from the Co-op at Garforth, sugar in blue two pounds bags, butter and lard, cut off the huge blocks back at the shop and weighed into pound sizes. The sugar and flour was kept in a warm cupboard in the hall based behind the fire. A Leeds Cooperative bill, 8lb sugar 1s-8d, ½lb tea 1s, ½lb lard 3½d, margarine 6d, 1lb currants 7d, 1lb-12ozs Groats 1s-3d, ½lb cocoa 11d, soap 6d, 1 fairy soap 5d, 2- 20 packet Gold Flake 2 shillings, 2 Palmolive soap 6d, 2oz yeast 1½d, 2lb bran £1-4d, 2lb sharps -£1.

We spring-cleaned every room in the summer. The carpets taken outside and scrubbed with an ammonia solution, hung on the washing line and banged with heavy sticks until the dust had cleared, the floors scrubbed and paintwork and curtains washed. For the windows we had a brush on the end of wood, which we made longer with extensions.

My mother cooked very nutritious meals, every week there was a rabbit or a pheasant to dress [that my father had shot and hung in the back kitchen for a few days], with her face turned away in disgust she made us laugh at the face she pulled, as she took the insides out. The resulting meals were delicious, with the dark red meat and thick brown gravy. We ate well in those years because of the dairy farm and my fathers home grown vegetables. My mother liked to come to the dances at Swillington too; She went to the Young Wives at Swillington Church and made some very good friends there. My mother loved company, and was such a good listener; the house was such a good place to be when she was there. As we grew up there was the warmth of a welcoming smile whenever we returned home, the same warmth too to all the visitors who came to our house. I remember having toothache and laying my head on her lap and the pain going away. She had favourite sayings like- 'don't cut off your nose to spite your face;' 'if you can't say nice things about anyone don't say anything;' 'don't fall out over children they will be friends again, long before you.' That advice was given when our children were born.

I remember plucking ducks one Christmas my dad had decided to get instead of the pig, my mother and I were not amused we were plucking until midnight, the kitchen floor was full of feathers and our fingers were so sore.

My mother was so proud of my sister Dorothy who trained to be a nurse at Leeds General Infirmary, we quickly got the housework done on her days off, so we could talk and listen to her. Training to be a nurse in those days in the 1950's was so hard with split days, and a month of night duty that made her really tired. I remember her having lots of boils, and she always suffered from Migraine. Dorothy must have gained much peace from coming home to my mother and the farm, the girls who trained with her visited too, they lived along way form their families, and enjoyed a bit of spoiling. My Mother had her teeth pulled out in the front room and had a miscarriage after Tommy was born, it was very serious but the fact was kept from us. My mother enjoyed the Yorkshire Shows at Harrogate and the Farmer's Union Dinners held in Leeds. When we were older, we stayed in to look after the farm whilst my father and mother enjoyed lovely days out to the Yorkshire Dales, to the Buttertubs, Skipton, Reeth and the countryside around Helmsley in North Yorkshire.

# Chapter Fourteen
# Time to Leave

I had spent the last five years after leaving school, working in the farmhouse and delivering the milk with my father around Foundry Lane. In 1955 my mother could cope, as the work was so much easier after the electricity had been put in. My mother and I decided that I could get a job away from the farm, so I started part-time work before Christmas at Marks and Spencers. I was twenty-one in the December and started work at Leeds Co-op in the January and worked there until I had David in 1961. Dorothy was nursing in Canada, Thomas worked on the farm, Shirley married Keith in September 1956 and I became engaged to Bob in the April on Bob's 21$^{st}$ birthday and we were married in October 1957. A quiet time for my Mam and Dad but the friends still visited them to play cards. I started work at the in Leeds Co-operative Society in the coat department of the large Department Store in Albion Street. The hours were long 8-30 to 6 o'clock with only Wednesday afternoon closing, my mother still had to have some help in the house. There was not enough to do in winter in the Coat department and I liked plenty to do. I applied to work at the food department at the Leeds Co-op Whitkirk. I could cycle there easily and enjoyed the work as we were always busy and we had lots of fun with Margaret, Norah and Pat, as we were a young crowd.

In 1955 Shirley, Derreen, Sheila and I went to Yarmouth on holiday and Bob came down on his motorbike. It took him four hours, setting off through the night. It was a scorching hot week.

In 1956 we went to Holland with Margaret and Ted; I was

working in Leeds at the Cooperative in Boar Lane selling coats and dresses at that time. We travelled overnight, and the signs of the war were still evident the houses all bombed and shelled. We stayed at Flushing; saw the film Roman holiday in a little village hall. We had a day in Rotterdam and looked round the shops there. The clothes were such bright colours. We saw Antwerp a beautiful city. We came back through Bruges. We had some days left so we stayed on the south coast and visited Canterbury Cathedral. Ted took us to Ten Downing Street. And we sat in St. James Park. I was so excited to see London.

Shirley married Keith Booth in September of 1956 at Swillington Church, Dorothy and I were bridesmaids, and they went to live on Dewsbury Road in my Mother's sister Alice's house, after she died. We missed Shirley but we went to tea and the pictures every Wednesday near their cosy house. We have always been such good friends as well as sisters.

We went to Blackpool with the Fountaines, Ronnie worked with Bob and was our best man at our wedding, and Cornwall with Shirley and Keith We travelled through Ilfracombe and stayed Bed and Breakfast at 10s and 6d a head, and then onto Newquay, and Torquay.

When we got back from that holiday Bob's Grandma Naylor, asked if we wanted to live with her in the very pretty house in Halton. It was a large airy house and it had a special garden and we bought it from her the next year and lived very happily in it for forty years.

Bob and I went to the vicar to arrange the marriage and on the 19th October 1957, we were married in my special Swillington Church with the bells ringing for us. I could not get over how it seemed that we were the only people in the church, as everyone was behind us. We went on honeymoon to Blackpool first and then Llandudno. The autumn in Wales was spectacular.

The next two years we travelled Scotland to John 0- Groats, Ullapool, and Mallaig a holiday in a tent, just big enough to crawl into, the weather was beautiful all week. The next year we went to Macduff on the edge of the sea. In 1960 we borrowed Bob's father's Vanguard car, and with Shirley and Keith toured France and Switzerland. On the way the Tour de France passed us. We were in Venice for Whit Sunday, the bells ringing out from the churches and processions of children in beautiful white dresses, as we travelled through Italy, along the French coast, through Monaco to Juan Les Pins, where we camped for a week. A really special holiday, it was so interesting to see so many different countries.

I became pregnant with David; Bob's paternal Grandparents died and were buried at Whitkirk. David was born on March 4th 1961, a special little baby who got a lot of spoiling and as a toddler, was so friendly and outgoing; he used to speak to everybody. Bob's Grandma Lucy died. Susan was born 16th May 1963. A quiet good little baby with bright ginger hair

In 1952 the land at Mount Pleasant was tested for Clay. The coal board mined coal beneath the farm and huge cracks appeared in the walls. Mr Dawson of Towton Hall near Tadcaster died and Mount Pleasant was sold to George Armitage of Robin Quarries, Robin Hood near Wakefield. The soil below the farm had excellent clay to make bricks and Armitage's Brickworks, was set up on the land. By 1961 it was quite a large concern selling excellent quality bricks all over the world.

It caused my father to worry about the farmland he would lose. These two factors worried my Dad so much; he had two very bad Strokes in 1961 that devastated him. Dorothy came home from Canada for a month to nurse him and because of the way they nursed in Canada [they did not like them to stay in bed,] my father improved, but always complained of a bad headache. It was a terrific strain on my mother, because he would not be left, believing he was about to have another stroke. My mother and father struggled on with Mount Pleasant Farm with the help of Dick Linley the farm manager, [Well Green Farm given up a few years earlier] for about two years, and then gave up the tenancy to Mr. Chapman from Austhorpe Hall, and my mother and Father moved to a house in Kingsway, Whitkirk.

The sale in 1962 from the livestock and equipment from Mount Pleasant Farm raised £3,540, including galvanised wash tank, milk cooler and sile, 3 Alfa Laval milking units, three Ferguson Tractors.

The Brickworks covered a large area of the fields in front and back of the farm. When the brick works were started at Mount Pleasant Farm in the 1960's, they discovered Iron Age Kilns and a late Bronze Age or Iron Age Roundhouse also a Roman corn-drying oven from the Roman Times. The Marshalls Clay Products now own it

Life should have been easier for my mother in her lovely modern sunny house; Bob and I lived in Halton and within walking distance. My mother missed not been able to entertain and fretted for a larger table. All she had was the little gate legged table that replaced it, eventually my father relented and bought a larger new one. My mother appreciated living near the shops and the buses, and thoroughly enjoyed her neighbours, who were very friendly people. By then Shirley and I had two children each which gave them a lot of pleasure.

After two years my mother had a heart attack rushing to in the hairdressers at Garforth, and taken to L.G.I., Doctor Robinson came and told us that there was no hope, but she walked in at teatime and lived another nine months. We persuaded the Doctor to say to my father, she needed a holiday and for the first time since she was married my mother enjoyed two weeks at Bridlington, with Auntie Dolly. Tommy joined them the second week with his car, whilst Bob and I stayed with my Dad.

In September my mother had another heart attack rushing for the bus to see my dad in hospital, and Dorothy, my eldest sister came home from Canada to look after them, she had been a nurse there for ten years. I was very grateful (there was no help then from Social Services) as I had David at four years and Susan at two year old, who were very lively children. Shirley and Keith had Christine and Alison the same age too, and Shirley was pregnant with Andrew. My mother died, on the 23rd December 1965 of a heart attack. The church at Whitkirk was packed at my mother's funeral, she was so well thought of, many of her friends from Swillington came. She was only fifty-eight.

My father died three months later in May 1966 at 65 years of age. He had not been in good health for five years having bladder cancer and the strokes. It was a very sad time for our family and friends to lose two special and caring people.

# Chapter Fifteen
# Dorothy and Thomas

Dorothy Mary Bowes was born at Foundry Mill Farm Seacroft Leeds on the 2nd August 1932. Her father was Aubrey Henry Robert Bowes 1901-1965, her mother Elsie Bowes [Britton] 1907–1964. Dorothy was a very bright ginger haired little girl. Dorothy was the eldest of four children Betty Margaret born 1934, Shirley Anne born 1937, and Thomas Aubrey born 1939. A close family.

Dorothy attended Swillington Primary School with teachers Miss Fozzard, Miss Stead, Mrs Bellwood, Miss Longbottom and Mrs Howarth. Dorothy passed the 11 plus and attended Rothwell Grammar School. Dorothy was a bright studious girl and she did extremely well. She left school at sixteen with good grades in the School Certificate, 6 Passes, one Credit and a Distinction. Dorothy loved school and was very good at Tennis. Dorothy had piano lessons. She loved to play tennis to and enjoyed the Theatre Royal in Leeds with Auntie Dolly. She had lovely holidays going abroad and when she was in Canada travelled extensively.

Dorothy at 13 years of age became ill with scarlet fever, a very serious illness, the house was fumigated and Dorothy was taken to the Isolation Hospital at Garforth cliff for six weeks. My mother and father were so upset. I remember them taking eggs and some of my mother's baking in a large basket to help Dorothy get better. Fresh eggs were prized for anyone in Hospital. The Hospital was built at Garforth Cliff built for Smallpox victims, Diphtheria, and Scarlet Fever 28 beds extended in 1937 at a cost of 18,000. The hospital was demolished in 1948. Whether she became interested in nursing at that stage I don't know. When she left school Dorothy worked for a while in Matthias Robinson's in Leeds.

In 1949 when Dorothy was seventeen, the Vicar of Swillington Saint Mary's Church, Mr. Cranmer wrote a letter to the Nurses Training School at Leeds General Infirmary applying for Dorothy who was accepted and started a period of Pre- Peaking at the Hospital For Women, Leeds before entering nurse Training at the LG I. in September 1950. The training extended over a period of four years during which period Dorothy was prepared for, and took the necessary examinations to qualify for Registration as a fully trained nurse under the General Nursing council of England and Wales.

Dorothy was admitted for a five months trial in which the first three months spent in the preliminary Training School where she received instruction in sick room cookery, elementary Anatomy and Physiology, Elementary Science, Surgical Cleanliness, Bandaging, Practical and Theoretical Nursing, so when she was admitted to the wards she had some acquaintance with the work she was called on to undertake. Examinations were held twice a year and the qualifying certificate given to Dorothy at the end of four years.

The salary Dorothy was paid 1st year £40, 2nd year, £45, 3rd year £50 and 4th year £60. £70 when she became a State Registered Nurse. In the 4th year the nurses who completed the Intermediate exam were designated ''Staff Nurses' and wore a distinctive uniform. Dorothy passed all the exams in 1952. After she was trained, there was a wide range of work, Dorothy could choose. Nurses who trained in her set achieved very good careers, Susan became the Matron at St James Hospital, and some nursed in Canada and Australia, and later became Health visitors. Dorothy arranged a reunion a year before she died and they came from all over the world.

The nurse's training School dates back from the opening of the present buildings in 1868. Before 1860 there was no organised or scientific training for nurses. The work of Florence Nightingale brought home to the nation the crying needs of the country at that time- namely the training and teaching of women wishful to carry on in her footsteps- to become State Registered Nurses.

Nursing has become one of the most honourable professions open to women The training extends over a period of four years during which period the nurse is prepared for, and takes the necessary examinations to qualify for Registration as a fully trained nurse under the General Nursing Council of England and Wales. The Matron whilst Dorothy was nursing was Miss Kathleen A. Raven, working at the Infirmary from June 1949 to 1957. She came from St. Bartholomew's Hospital. She had 540 nurses in her care. She brought many improvements in the nursing of patients and the well being of her staff. Miss Raven started the Assistant Nurse Training School at The Ida and Robert Arthington Hospital and introduced 'Beaux 'parlours'. She married Professor J.T. Ingram the Physician in charge of the Dept of Dermatology from 1927 to 1959.

Life on the ward was very busy. In those days student nurses undertook all sorts of jobs including filling in for cleaning staff. There were no vacuum cleaners or refrigerators. Bedpans and bottles had to be soaked in disinfectant. A typical ward in 1946 was rather drab and had a coal fire in the middle, which needed tending. The old screens had no wheels and had to be carried bodily around the ward. Milk was delivered to the ward daily in a large churn. Junior nurses had to count and bag all the dirty bed linen and send any worn items for repair. It was a crime to break any crockery or thermometers, and explanations had to be given before an item replaced. Syringes and needles were boiled before use and were in short supply, as disposables had not been invented. New needles were not issued without the permission of the pharmacist. Christian names were never used

I remember there was a list of things Dorothy had to take including a radio and the cost amounted to £100. Dorothy lived in at nurses home in Clarendon Road. She trained with a very nice set of girls, who always stayed friends. I remember her having Glandular Fever, and lots of boils on her neck and a nasty one in her ear. They all worked very long hours in split shifts in the morning, hours off in the afternoon, and back on at night. They had to work a month of nights, which Dorothy found very hard. When Dorothy came home she was very tired. She suffered from Migraine and seemed to get an attack on the first morning after she had been on night duty. After three years training at the L.G. I. she passed the exams, to be a qualified S.R N. and RGN. She spent a year as a Staff Nurse on a General Medical Ward, and then went south to undertake her Midwifery training at the Middlesex hospital, [Midwifery training started in 1930's] then at the Private clinic in London where she helped to nurse Merle Oberon, a famous actress at the time.

Dorothy with two friends Jo and Chris, nursed in Canada for ten years in Calgary, Toronto and Red Lake where she nursed the Indian people in the Northern Territory, now called Native Canadians now. She travelled extensively in Canada. She thoroughly enjoyed not only the landscape of Canada but also the people of Canada and the whole way of life

Dorothy came home in September to nurse my Mother who had had a heart attack in March 1964 she died at Christmas and father had Cancer, and he died in three months after in 1965. Dorothy lived at 6 Kingsway with Thomas and after staying with Thomas for two years; Dorothy bought a bungalow at Garforth where Bob and I live now. Health visitor training at Leeds University was the next step in her career and work in which she found great satisfaction and fulfilment especially on specialising and becoming a Diabetic Liaison Officer within the Western District at Leeds General Infimary where she had trained. She was a very caring person and was appreciated by the children who had Diabetes; that she nursed in the last years of nursing.

This was work that she thoroughly enjoyed until Health problems necessitated her early retirement. She had a heart valve replaced at Killingbeck Hospital, which caused liver problems and spent many months in and out of hospital.

Unfortunately in her years of retirement were six years of gradual but relentless deterioration in health. This was however borne with great courage, stiff discipline and cheerfulness. Dorothy made every effort to live it to the full, pursuing her interests in the appreciation of nature and the Arts-especially music. Her time absorbing hobby was painting on China, she attended lessons in Barwick and painted some lovely plates shared amongst the family, and painted on china a beautiful dinner set for her niece Christine. It was an art in which she became increasingly proficient and a source of great pleasure to her. Dorothy loved music and went to the concerts at Leeds Town Hall and the theatres in Leeds. When she died she was sadly missed by Shirley and I and our families and to the many friends to whom she was always loyal, kind and at the ready in times of need. I had many beautiful days shopping in Harrogate, Bradford and Leeds I only worked part time and really enjoyed these special days. She was a marvellous Aunt to the children especially Andrew the youngest of them all.

Dorothy sent this huge tractor from Canada for our son David who was her godson. It was bright orange and he could sit on it. I gave her a new navy and white dress when she returned back to Canada to wear on the ship she looked very pretty After a few months back came a lovely warm blue anorak in return that I wore loads. I loved reading the letters she sent. There was a caring Telegram she sent when we got married and the lovely letter after David was born, she was so sorry to have missed them both. The cost of travel from Canada to England was a great sum of money

# Thomas

Thomas was the youngest child of Aubrey and Elsie Bowes, and the brother of Dorothy, Shirley and myself. He was born 5th May 1939. His birth was greatly celebrated, as my father was so pleased to have a son. I remember we had a christening party and all the relations came, and we played rounders in the yard. We had only moved to Mount Pleasant Farm recently. Soon after moving the horse Tommy slipped into a ditch in the field below the farm and broke a leg and had to be shot, with great sadness. Our brother was born soon after and they named him Thomas, it was a joke in the family that he had been named after the horse, but Thomas is a family name anyway. We thought the world of Thomas and he was spoilt and by the time he was three he was full of mischief, stubborn, with a quirky sense of humour, and the bane of my father's life. When Thomas was seven year old he was playing in front of the fire, even though we had a big fireguard, the big double pan slipped on the fire and the hot water scalded his forearm badly. He had the scar all his life. I can still remember my father shouting at my mother, for letting Thomas play near the fire. In the forties, scalds were very serious and paraffin gauze dressings were all they could use to treat a scald, and took many months to heal.

Thomas went to Castleford Modern School. The children were a bit naughty and Thomas came home with tales of the teacher throwing a blackboard rubber at a pupil, and the pupil throwing it back, a thing unheard of in Rothwell Grammar School. Thomas loved cricket and played all the time, whenever he could in the fields, mainly with Shirley, and at school.

It was a cricket ball hitting his hipbone and dislodging a bone that caused his first spell in the Leeds General Infirmary. Thomas had terrible pain and screamed out in the night [1956], the doctor said it was rheumatism, but he was in such pain they admitted him to Leeds General Infirmary, the x-rays showed the displaced bone. The Doctors had weights put on his legs and he spent many months in hospital He was sixteen at the time. Thomas worked on the farm when his leg and hip was better. It was a dairy farm with the cows to be milked twice a day. My father employed six men besides Thomas. My father was very protective and would not let us go where it was dangerous on the farm.

When Thomas was sixteen he bought a bright blue scooter, his pride and joy, he rode many miles around the countryside. Shirley and Keith Booth were married at Swillington Church in 1956 and went to live at Parkside Parade on Dewsbury Road and Bob and I married 1957 and went to live with Bob's grandma Lucy Naylor in Halton.

One night Thomas was riding the scooter early after finishing work. He came off the scooter and hit his head, without a crash helmet and was knocked unconscious. A bus saw him in the headlights. Thomas was rushed to hospital with no means of identification on him. My father and mother because he had gone out without his tea or getting changed, became very worried, and drove to our houses to see if he was there, and any other place he might be. Finally news filtered through that there had been an accident at Swillington, my father rang the hospital. The staffs were so cross that it had taken so long to ring. Thomas was bleeding from his ears and nose and dangerously ill, and needed an operation immediately. At first my father would not agree, but my sister Dorothy, who was training at the L.G.I. at the time, persuaded him to sign the forms. It was a very anxious time for the family and Thomas was in danger. Shirley and I had compassionate leave from work. Thomas came round with one eye shut and the other staring at you, his speech very bad. After he came home he spent his time listening to music in the front room and he was about a year before he worked on the farm again. He was very handsome in the summer when he turned a lovely brown.

Thomas bought a motorbike and sidecar believing it to be safer. My mother and dad had gone for a ride to the Yorkshire Dales one Sunday in 1960 and we had to break the news, that Thomas had again had an accident on the Wakefield Road, below the farm, he had overtaken and run into another car. Thomas had broken both his legs and his wrist. After another six months, lots of pain, resetting of the bones in his legs, and his wrist and with so many journeys and anxious hours to Leeds Infirmary and the Ida hospital for my mother and dad, he came home. I remember my mother's distress when they took the pot from his legs and they were full of sores. Thomas hardly complained, and again found consolation in his music and eventually started work on the farm.

In 1961 he moved to Kingsway Whitkirk, Thomas passed his driving test and got a job delivering parcels to the airports. He loved the job but was often late home which worried my mother. My mother had the Heart Attack in the March and my sister Dorothy finished work in Canada where she had worked for ten years, as a R.G.N. nurse working in Calgary Red Lake and Toronto, to come home in the September before my mother and father died, and nursed them both. Dorothy stayed with Thomas. Dorothy trained to be a Health Visitor at the University in Leeds, and afterwards when Thomas could cope on his own,

Dorothy moved to a bungalow at Garforth where we now live.

Thomas, because of the operation on his head began having epileptic fits but they were controlled with tablets, and after another spell off work and because he was not allowed to drive, he found a job with E.J. Arnold in Leeds and was very happy there. During this time he was beaten up in Leeds, and the hospital thought he had lost the sight in his eye, but mercifully the eye was safe, but his face was all bruised and his nose broken.

When he was in his early fifties he had a hip replacement and retired on sickness grounds, and received a mobility car which gave him so much pleasure, as he could only manage a few steps with much pain, but miraculously said he did not have much pain sitting down. Thomas lived on his own and was so independent he would not have a telephone or any help. He loved to go to Bournemouth every year for his holidays to the same address, they really thought a lot about him and made him feel so welcome. Bob and I had a golden retriever, which he thought the world of, and loved to tease from his chair, but I was always frightened that Ben would be too boisterous and hurt him. But they had a wonderful friendship. Our children and grandchildren thought the world of him, a special uncle.

Thomas died very quietly within a few hours of a heart attack when he was fifty-seven, on 25th May 1996. The doctor said he had been lucky to live to that age, with all that he had suffered all his life. Thomas was a remarkable kind gentleman, who never complained, always a smile and a welcome when you visited him.

# Chapter Sixteen
# The Marson Family

Dorothy Mary Marson was born 17 May 1905, and lived at Armley before they moved to 18 The Mount in the 1920's. Her father was Samuel George Naylor from 34 Skilbeck Street, New Wortley and was in later life the Stationmaster at Poole station. Her mother was Lucy Naylor, whose Father was James Naylor Horsekeeper, 7 Redshaw Road, Armley Her sister called Edna, a shorthand typist who was married to Mike who died of appendicitis just after the war. They had a son Michael who married Jennie they lived at Hemel Hempstead and afterwards moved to Pickering, North Yorkshire.

Dorothy had a brother Ronald who was a sea captain he was married to Margaret and they had a daughter named Janet and they lived next door to Bob's mother and dad. They now live at Kendal.

Rowland Marson whose father was William Henry Marson 24th October 1869-23rd March 1960 from 25 Stamford Street Armley. His mother was Lily Sowden, who died in 1959 who lived at 20 Argyle Street Armley. Bob's grandparents on his father's side were butchers. They had a butcher's shop Sowden's at Chapel Allerton. They were a lovely homely couple that lived in Crossgates in 3 Poplar Avenue. Bob used to cut their grass for them. Grandpa Marson was a very pleasant slight man with lots of white hair, a courteous well-mannered gentleman who did the shopping for the house bound in their street. He gave a very good speech at our wedding. He was ninety-two at the time. Bob's father visited them every Friday for his tea, which at the time I thought was a lovely idea. Grandma Marson was a tiny lady who suffered from arthritis, a wonderful cook and it was nice to visit them. They were very strong Methodists at the Crossgates Church. They died within a few months of each other, his Grandma first of Cancer, and Grandpa Marson fell and broke his hip and died at 28 Austhorpe Avenue in 1960. He was 93 years old and his grandma 89 years old.

Bob's father Rowland was a soldier in the First World War; he served in France and was gassed in the war. He was an air-raid warden in the 2nd War. He was a very tall striking man; he loved playing bowls in the summer at Manston Park and snooker, all the winter months in the room behind the Methodist Church in Crossgates after he retired. After his father died Rowland bought a Standard Vanguard, which brought them a lot of pleasure. He suffered from Arthritis and was always very breathless, perhaps from the gas in the First World War.

Bob's Grandpa and his Father both worked for the Gas Board, and they were reported in the Yorkshire Post as two generations of the same family, drawing pension at the same time. His arthritis was so painful; he sat many an hour watching T.V. and could hardly manage the path to the gate. He lived to eighty years, always a very pleasant gentleman; he always made you feel so welcome. He loved the grandchildren to come and made such a fuss of David, Susan, Richard and Heather. My special sister in law Joan and I took turns to make a meal every fortnight, which all the family enjoyed, for over thirty years. We had special Christmas, birthdays and anniversaries together too.

Bob's mother worked at the Post Office and learnt the Morse code and used to pass messages to Bob's Father when they were courting. She was a very good cook and made special chocolate cakes ginger biscuits and cocoanut macaroons. They lived all their married life at Authored Avenue. Bob's Mother too, lived to eighty years.

Bob's mother Dorothy, dad Rowland, brother John and his wife Joan are buried in Whitkirk Churchyard. Bob's grandparents, Lucy and Samuel Naylor and William and Lily Marson are buried there too.

# Chapter Seventeen
# John Smeaton

John Smeaton was born at Austhorpe Lodge Leeds 15. On the 8th June 1724 and died 28th October 1792 age 68 years. The house is quite near Templenewsam Estate His father was a respectable attorney. He was of middle stature broad and strongly made and a constitution of great vigour, a very straightforward man.

He designed the water wheel for Foundry Mill Farm at Seacroft Leeds along with 43 water mills and numerous windmills.

He was happiest when he had a cutting tool to make imitations of houses, pumps and windmills. Even when he was quite tiny he made circles and squares. After watching the operations of some wheelwrights, he was seen fixing a rude likeness of a windmill on top of his father's barn. After watching men refixing the village pump he obtained a piece of bored pipe and fashioned it into a working pump, which actually raised water. He attended Leeds Grammar School .He was very good in Geometry and Arithmetic.

He watched some mechanics erect a fire engine as a steam engine. It was called for the purpose of pumping of pumping water from the Garforth Coal mines. Carefully examining their methods he constructed a miniature engine at home. He quickly emptied a fishpond near his home.

By the time he was fifteen he had made a turning lathe, on which he turned ivory and wood and it was his delight to make little boxes and other articles of his own manufacture to give to his friends. He also learned to work in metals, which he forged without any assistance; and by the time he was eighteen he handled his tools as dexterously as any regular smith and joiner. He forged iron and steel melted his metal. He had tools of every sort for working in wood ivory and metals. He had made a lathe by which he cut a perpetual screw in brass, which was the invention of Mr. Hindley of York. He spent many a night at his house

When John Smeaton was sixteen he left school he school and entered his fathers' office copying dreary legal documents and acquiring a knowledge of law to fit him for an attorney's profession.

1742 he was sent to London and entered the services of a philosophical instrument maker. He read industriously the principles of theoretically science. He sought the society of educated men. He attended the meetings and lectures of the Royal Society.

John Smeaton lived all his life at Austhorpe Leeds. He erected an Atelier, a study and an observatory all in one. A form of a square tower four stories high. The ground floor was the forge, first floor his lathe, the third his study the fourth, a lumber-room and attic. From the little turreted staircase on the top led to a door onto the leads. A vane fixed on the summit was so arranged that it set in motion the hands of a dial on the ceiling and showed at any moment the direction of the wind.

He started in business in 1750 when he was only 26yrs old and read a paper before the Royal Society on certain improvements by Himself and Dr. Knight in the mariners compass.

In1751 he invented a machine to measure a ships way at sea. He made improvements in the air pump. He made a modification in ship's tackle by means of a pulley so that one man could easily raise a ton weight. He describes certain experiments that had been made with Captain Savary's steam engine, a precursor of James Watt.

He was engaged in researches into "the Natural Powers of Water and Wind to Turn Mills and other Machines depending on a Circular Motion which gained him the Royal Society's Gold Medal, almost the highest honour a man of science can receive in England.

John Smeaton studied French 1754 traversed Holland and Belgium, the great sea sluices at Brill and Helvoetsluys and made huge notes and the information was of great use in his after labours as a canal and harbour engineer.

When John Smeaton was thirty-two years of age he was asked to design the Eddystone Lighthouse in 1755. The Trinity House Corporation was determined to erect another lighthouse and instructed the work to a mathematical instrument maker John Smeaton, who had gained a reputation as an ingenious mechanical engineer.

The lighthouse is 14 miles southwest of Plymouth, on a reef called the Eddystone in a line with Lizard Head in Cornwall and Start point in Devonshire. A perilous obstruction not only in the waterway which leads to South Devon but the track of all vessels entering or leaving the English Channel. It is frequented by a greater number of ships than any other part of the wide ocean. Several low jagged ridges of rocks stand out. John Smeaton decided that the structures of his predecessors had both been deficient in weight he declared his intention therefore of raising a fabric of such solidarity, that the sea should give way to it, and not it to the sea, and build it entirely of stone

Work began in June 1757 with 46 courses of masonry, elevation 70ft.

It was completed in 1759.

1764 John Smeaton was appointed the receiver of Derwentwater Estates.

1760 The Magistrates for Dumfries consulted him on the improvement of the Nitts

*Lockage of the river Wear*
*The opening up of the navigation of the Chelmar to Chelmsford*
*River Don at Doncaster*
*The Devon river in Cluckmannanshire.*
*Tetney Haven near Louth.*
*Extensive repairs of the dams and locks to the River Calder.*
*Extensive works on the River Aire from Leeds to its junction with*
*The Ouse.*
*Lots of Drainage to the Fens and Rivers*
*1763 Corporation of London called upon him to advise improving*
*and widening the Old London Bridge [foundations as minutely as*
*possible] he advised the Corporation to repurchase the stones of*
*the city gates and cast them into the river outside the startings or*
*buttresses to protect them from the tide.*
*He contributed papers on astronomical subjects to the Royal*
*Society.*
*John Smeaton- there was scarcely a bridge or a canal that he did*
*not restore and widen.*
*The bridge at Perth 1772*
*Coldstream -River Tweed cost 6,000 pounds had 5 arches in 1766*
*The bridge at Banff 7 arches 410 ft and 20ft width.*
*He improved the water supply of Edinburgh.*
*Strengthened the bridge at Glasgow*
*Forth and Clyde Canal in 1768. It was 38 miles long, 39 locks.*
*Elevation of 156ft, depth 8ft. Cost of 200,000 pounds.*
*He built The Bridge at Hexham and was destroyed in a violent*
*storm. The only failure.*
*The Harbour at St. Ives. Whitehaven. Workington Bristol Rye*
*Christchurch and Dover. Yarmouth Lynn Scarborough,*
*Sunderland, Ramsgate, Sandwich- harbour of safe refuge.*
*1749 The harbour at Ramsgate it was the best upon the South*
*Coast. - 42 acres and piers extending 310 ft into the sea an*
*opening of 200ft.*

*1770 John Smeaton altered Aberdeen, Portpatrick and Eyemouth.*
*Spurn Point Lighthouse.*
*The National Dockyards at Portsmouth and Plymouth.*

He enjoyed huge success as a capable engineer he crowded in an extraordinary amount of good and useful achievement into his active life, and whatever he did was so carefully done as never to repair, patching or redoing.

There was scarcely a bridge or a canal in the kingdom that he did not restore, enlarge or some way improve.

When a new water company was started to supply some hitherto unprovided town or district, John Smeaton was called upon as consulting engineer to the town.

Landowners to drain their estate.

Coalowners to work their mines more safely and efficiently. There seems to have been no department or engineering Science in which he was not largely and successfully employed. It was said of him that he was ready to supply a design of any new machine, from a fire bucket, or a ship's pump to a turning lathe or a steam engine. His genius was equally at home with a small thing as with great. Whatever he designed was remarkable for the finish and neatness of execution.

The water-pumping engine that was erected for Lord Irwin at Templenewsam near his home at Austhorpe Leeds, to pump water for the supply of the mansion, is an admirable piece of workmanship and continues to this day.

Water power was used for nearly all purposes for which steam is now applied such as grinding flour, sawing wood, boring and hammering iron, fulling cloth, rolling cloth, rolling copper and driving all kinds of machinery.

Steam engines developing, he erected a steam engine, near Austhorpe on Newcomen's principle. His Chacewater engine 150 horsepower was looked on as one of the best. It was surpassed by James Watt's condensing machine.

No engineering works of any importance were undertaken without his advice. He was constantly consulted in Parliament, but it was studied thoroughly before he gave advice.

John Smeaton died 28th October 1792. He is interred with his forefathers in Whitkirk Church Leeds. On the North wall, near the altar there is erected a memorial to his work as an engineer, a tablet with the moulding of the Eddystone Lighthouse, which is situated near Plymouth.

A memorial Plaque is in the North Aisle of the Nave of Westminster Abbey in London to John Smeaton.

John Smeaton possessed the gift of fluent and clear description. He could make difficult points of engineering science intelligible even to non-professional readers or hearers. In the courts of law he was frequently complimented by Lord Mansfield and the other judges for the light he ingeniously threw upon obtuse and very difficult subjects. His secret was his thorough Knowledge of what he wrote and spoke about. He was always thorough and hence always spoke with the decision and confidence of a master.